The Best Slow Cooker Recipes

Publications International, Ltd.
Favorite Brand Name Recipes at www.fbnr.com

Pictured on the front cover *(clockwise from top right):* Cajun-Style Country Ribs *(page 88),* Caribbean Sweet Potato & Bean Stew *(page 26),* Slow Cooker Steak Fajitas *(page 96)* and Three-Bean Mole Chili *(page 6).*
Pictured on the back cover: Italian-Style Sausage with Rice *(page 84).*

ISBN-13: 978-1-4127-2160-8
ISBN-10: 1-4127-2160-1

Library of Congress Control Number: 2004115117

Manufactured in China.

8 7 6 5 4 3 2 1

Preparation/Cooking Times: Preparation times are based on the approximate amount of time required to assemble the recipe before cooking, baking, chilling or serving. These times include preparation steps such as measuring, chopping and mixing. The fact that some preparations and cooking can be done simultaneously is taken into account. Preparation of optional ingredients and serving suggestions is not included.

CONTENTS

The Slow Cooker

History

Slow cookers were introduced in the 1970's; their popularity was renewed in the mid-1990's and continues into the present day. Considering the hectic pace of today's lifestyles, it's no wonder so many people have rediscovered this time-saving kitchen appliance. Spend a few minutes preparing the ingredients, or buy precut meat and vegetables, so all you have to do is place them right in the slow cooker and relax. The low heat and long cooking times take the stress out of meal preparation. Leave for work or a day of leisure and come home to a hot, delicious meal.

There are two types of slow cookers. The most common models have heat coils circling the crockery inset, allowing heat to surround the food and cook evenly. Two settings, LOW (about 200°F) and HIGH (about 300°F) regulate cooking temperatures. One hour on HIGH equals 2 to $2^1/_2$ hours on LOW. Less common models have heat coils on the bottom. If you own this type, consult your manufacturer's instructions for advice on converting the recipes in this publication.

Tips for Successful Slow Cooking

Filling the Slow Cooker
Manufacturers recommend that slow cookers should be one-half to three-quarters full for best results.

Keeping the Lid On
A slow cooker can take as long as twenty minutes to regain heat lost when the cover is removed. If the recipe calls for stirring or checking the dish near the end of the cooking time, replace the cover as quickly as you can. Otherwise, resist the urge to remove the cover.

Cleaning the Slow Cooker
Always follow the manufacturer's instructions. To make cleanup even easier, spray the slow cooker with nonstick cooking spray before adding ingredients.

Tasting It
You will always want to taste the finished dish before serving. Seasonings often need to be adjusted to your preferences.

Converting Recipes
If you would like to adapt your own favorite recipe to a slow cooker, you'll need to follow a few guidelines. First, try to find a similar slow cooker recipe. Take note of the cooking times, amount of liquid, and quantity and size of meat and vegetable pieces. The slow cooker captures moisture, so you will want to reduce the amount of liquid, often by as much as half. Add dairy products toward the end of the cooking time so they do not curdle.

Selecting Meat
Keep in mind that you can, and in fact should, use tougher, inexpensive cuts of meat. Top-quality cuts, such as loin chops or filet mignon, fall apart during long cooking periods and therefore are not good choices to use in the slow cooker. You will be amazed to find that even the toughest cuts of meat will come out fork-tender and flavorful.

Reducing the Fat
The slow cooker can help you make low-fat meals because you will not be cooking in fat. And tougher, inexpensive cuts of meat have less fat than the prime cuts. Many of the recipes even call for trimming the excess fat from the meat before cooking.

Chicken skin tends to shrivel and curl in the slow cooker, so most recipes call for skinless chicken. If you use skin-on pieces, brown them before adding them to the slow cooker.

You can also remove most of the fat from accumulated juices and soups. The simplest way is to refrigerate the liquid for several hours or overnight. The fat will float to the top and congeal for easy removal. If you plan to serve the liquid right away, ladle it into a bowl or measuring cup. Let it stand about 5 minutes so the fat can rise to the surface. Skim with a large spoon. You can also lightly pull a sheet of clean paper towel over the surface, letting it absorb the fat.

Cutting Vegetables
Vegetables often take longer to cook than meats. Cut vegetables into small, thin pieces and place them near the bottom or sides of the slow cooker. Pay careful attention to the recipe instructions in order to cut vegetables to the proper size so they will cook in the amount of time given.

By taking note of these simple slow-cooker tips, you will be preparing wonderful slow cooker recipes with the minimum of effort.

SOUPS, STEWS & CHILIS

Three-Bean Mole Chili

Prep Time: *10 minutes* / **Cook Time:** *5 to 6 hours*

1 can (15 ounces) pinto beans, rinsed and drained
1 can (15 ounces) chili beans in spicy sauce, undrained
1 can (15 ounces) black beans, rinsed and drained
1 can (14½ ounces) Mexican or chili-style diced tomatoes, undrained
1 large green bell pepper, diced
1 small onion, diced
½ cup beef, chicken or vegetable broth
¼ cup prepared mole paste*
2 teaspoons ground cumin
2 teaspoons chili powder
2 teaspoons minced garlic
2 teaspoons ground coriander (optional)
   Toppings: crushed tortilla chips, chopped fresh cilantro or shredded cheese

Mole paste is available in the Mexican section of large supermarkets or in specialty markets.

Slow Cooker Directions
1. Combine beans, tomatoes with juice, bell pepper, onion, broth, mole, cumin, chili powder, garlic and coriander, if desired, in slow cooker; mix well.

2. Cover; cook on LOW 5 to 6 hours or until vegetables are tender.

3. Place toppings in small bowls. Serve hot chili with toppings.

Makes 4 to 6 servings

Simple Turkey Soup

2 pounds ground turkey, cooked and drained
1 can (28 ounces) whole tomatoes, undrained
2 cans (14 ounces each) beef broth
1 bag (16 ounces) frozen mixed soup vegetables (such as carrots, beans, okra, corn or onion)
½ cup uncooked barley
1 teaspoon salt
1 teaspoon dried thyme leaves
½ teaspoon ground coriander
Black pepper

Slow Cooker Directions

Combine all ingredients in slow cooker. Add water to cover. Cover; cook on HIGH 3 to 4 hours or until barley and vegetables are tender.

Makes 8 servings

COOK'S TIP

This soup is very easy to make! Try adding other frozen or canned vegetables or diced potatoes. Sliced, diced or stewed tomatoes can be substituted for the whole tomatoes. For a large crowd, add corn and serve with corn bread.

Simple Turkey Soup

Rustic Vegetable Soup

1 jar (16 ounces) picante sauce
1 package (10 ounces) frozen mixed vegetables, thawed
1 package (10 ounces) frozen cut green beans, thawed
1 can (10 ounces) condensed beef broth, undiluted
1 to 2 baking potatoes, cut into ½-inch pieces
1 medium green bell pepper, chopped
½ teaspoon sugar
¼ cup finely chopped fresh parsley

Slow Cooker Directions

Combine all ingredients except parsley in slow cooker. Cover; cook on LOW 8 hours or on HIGH 4 hours. Stir in parsley; serve.   *Makes 8 servings*

Easy Corn Chowder

Prep Time: *15 minutes* / **Cook Time:** *7 to 8 hours*

2 cans (14½ ounces each) chicken broth
1 bag (16 ounces) frozen corn kernels
3 small potatoes, peeled and cut into ½-inch pieces
1 red bell pepper, diced
1 medium onion, diced
1 rib celery, sliced
½ teaspoon salt
½ teaspoon black pepper
¼ teaspoon ground coriander
½ cup heavy cream
8 slices bacon, crisp-cooked and crumbled (optional)

Slow Cooker Directions

1. Place broth, corn, potatoes, bell pepper, onion, celery, salt, black pepper and coriander into slow cooker. Cover; cook on LOW 7 to 8 hours.

2. Partially mash soup mixture with potato masher to thicken. Stir in cream; cook on HIGH, uncovered, until hot. Adjust seasonings, if desired. Garnish with bacon, if desired.   *Makes 6 servings*

Rustic Vegetable Soup

Red Bean Soup with Andouille Sausage

2 tablespoons unsalted butter
1 large onion, diced
3 stalks celery, diced
2 large cloves garlic, chopped
1 ham hock
8 cups chicken stock
1½ cups dried red kidney beans, soaked in cold water 1 hour, rinsed and drained
1 bay leaf
1 pound andouille smoked sausage or other pork sausage, cut into ½-inch pieces
1 sweet potato, diced
2 parsnips, diced
   Salt and black pepper to taste

Slow Cooker Directions

1. Melt butter in large saucepan over medium heat. Add onion, celery and garlic. Cook and stir 5 minutes; add to slow cooker along with ham hock, chicken stock, kidney beans and bay leaf. Cover; cook on HIGH 2 hours.

2. Remove ham hock and discard. Cover; cook 2 hours more.

3. Add sausage, potato and parsnips. Cover; cook 30 minutes more or until kidney beans are soft. Season with salt and pepper.   *Makes 6 to 8 servings*

Note: Use a 6-quart slow cooker for this recipe. If using a smaller slow cooker, cut recipe ingredients in half.

Red Bean Soup with Andouille Sausage

Mushroom Barley Stew

Prep Time: *10 minutes* / **Cook Time:** *6 to 7 hours*

1 tablespoon olive oil
1 medium onion, finely chopped
1 cup chopped carrots (about 2 medium carrots)
1 clove garlic, minced
1 cup uncooked pearl barley
1 cup dried wild mushrooms, broken into pieces
1 teaspoon salt
½ teaspoon dried thyme leaves
½ teaspoon black pepper
5 cups vegetable broth

Slow Cooker Directions

1. Heat oil in medium skillet over medium-high heat. Add onion, carrots and garlic; cook and stir 5 minutes or until tender. Place in slow cooker.

2. Add barley, mushrooms, salt, thyme and pepper to slow cooker. Stir in broth.

3. Cover; cook on LOW 6 to 7 hours. Adjust seasonings, if desired.

Makes 4 to 6 servings

COOK'S TIP

To turn this thick robust stew into a soup,
add 2 to 3 additional cups of broth.
Cook the same length of time.

Mushroom Barley Stew

Double-Hearty, Double-Quick Veggie Chili

2 cans (15½ ounces each) dark kidney beans, rinsed and drained

1 package (16 ounces) frozen bell pepper stir-fry mixture *or* 2 bell peppers, chopped

1 cup frozen corn kernels

1 can (14½ ounces) diced tomatoes with peppers, celery and onions, undrained

3 tablespoons chili powder or to taste

2 teaspoons sugar

2 teaspoons ground cumin, divided

½ teaspoon salt

1 tablespoon extra virgin olive oil

Sour cream (optional)

Chopped fresh cilantro (optional)

Slow Cooker Directions

1. In colander, combine beans, bell pepper mixture and corn. Run under cold water until beans and vegetables are well rinsed. Shake off excess water; place in slow cooker. Add tomatoes with juice, chili powder, sugar and 1½ teaspoons cumin.

2. Cover; cook on LOW 5 hours or on HIGH 3 hours.

3. Stir in salt, remaining ½ teaspoon cumin and olive oil. Serve with sour cream and cilantro, if desired. *Makes 4 to 6 servings*

Note: If using fresh bell peppers, add 1 small onion, chopped.

Double-Hearty, Double-Quick Veggie Chili

Mediterranean Lentil Soup

2 tablespoons olive oil

1 large onion, diced

1 stalk celery, chopped

2 large cloves garlic, finely minced

1 can (28 ounces) peeled whole plum tomatoes, drained and chopped

1½ cups dried lentils, soaked in cold water 1 hour, rinsed and drained*

1 tablespoon tomato paste

1½ teaspoons dried thyme leaves

6 cups beef broth

2 bay leaves

Vinaigrette

¾ cup packed fresh basil leaves

⅓ cup olive oil

2 tablespoons minced fresh parsley leaves

2 tablespoons red wine vinegar

Salt and black pepper to taste

Add 1 to 2 hours to cooking time if you do not soak lentils before cooking.

Slow Cooker Directions

1. Place all ingredients except vinaigrette in slow cooker. Stir to combine; cover and cook on LOW 8 hours or on HIGH 4 hours or until lentils are soft.

2. While soup is simmering, prepare vinaigrette. Combine basil, ⅓ cup olive oil, parsley and vinegar in blender or food processor. Process on high speed until smooth. Stir vinaigrette into soup just before serving. Season with salt and pepper. *Makes 4 to 6 servings*

Mediterranean Lentil Soup

Peppery Potato Soup

Prep Time: *15 minutes* / **Cook Time:** *6 to 8 hours*

2 cans (14½ ounces each) chicken broth
4 small baking potatoes, halved and sliced
1 large onion, quartered and sliced
1 rib celery with leaves, sliced
¼ cup all-purpose flour
¾ teaspoon black pepper
½ teaspoon salt
1 cup half-and-half
1 tablespoon butter
   Celery leaves and fresh parsley (optional)

Slow Cooker Directions

1. Combine broth, potatoes, onion, celery, flour, pepper and salt in slow cooker; mix well. Cover; cook on LOW 6 to 7½ hours.

2. Stir in half-and-half; cover and continue to cook 1 hour.

3. Remove slow cooker lid. Slightly crush potato mixture with potato masher. Continue to cook, uncovered, an additional 30 minutes until slightly thickened. Just before serving, stir in butter. Garnish with celery leaves and parsley, if desired.   *Makes 6 (1¼-cup) servings*

Peppery Potato Soup

Winter's Best Bean Soup

Prep Time: *15 minutes* / **Cook Time:** *8 hours*

  6 ounces bacon, diced
 10 cups chicken broth
  3 cans (15 ounces each) Great Northern beans, drained
  1 can (14½ ounces) diced tomatoes, undrained
  1 package (10 ounces) frozen sliced or diced carrots
  1 large onion, chopped
  2 teaspoons minced garlic
  1 fresh rosemary sprig *or* 1 teaspoon dried rosemary leaves
  1 teaspoon black pepper

Slow Cooker Directions

1. Cook bacon in medium skillet over medium-high heat just until cooked; drain and transfer to slow cooker. Add remaining ingredients.

2. Cover; cook on LOW 8 hours or until beans are tender. Remove rosemary sprig and mince leaves before serving.   *Makes 8 to 10 servings*

Serving Suggestion: Place slices of toasted Italian bread in bottom of individual soup bowls. Drizzle with olive oil. Pour soup over bread and serve.

Slow Cooker Cheese Soup

  4 cups (16 ounces) shredded Cheddar cheese
  2 cans (10¾ ounces each) condensed cream of celery soup, undiluted
  1 teaspoon paprika
  1 teaspoon Worcestershire sauce
 1¼ cups half-and-half
    Salt and black pepper

Slow Cooker Directions

1. Combine cheese, soup, paprika and Worcestershire sauce in slow cooker.

2. Cover; cook on LOW 2 to 3 hours.

3. Add half-and-half; stir to combine. Cover; cook another 20 minutes. Season with salt and pepper to taste. Garnish as desired.   *Makes 4 servings*

Winter's Best Bean Soup

Lamb Stew

1 large onion, chopped
2 to 3 tablespoons plus 1½ teaspoons bacon fat or olive oil, divided
½ cup all-purpose flour
2 teaspoons salt
1 teaspoon black pepper
3 pounds boneless lamb for stew, cut into 2- to 2½-inch pieces
2 tablespoons sugar, divided
3 cans (14½ ounces each) beef broth
3 tablespoons tomato paste
4 cloves garlic, chopped
1 tablespoon dried thyme leaves
1 tablespoon fresh chopped rosemary leaves
2 bay leaves
1 pound carrots, peeled and cut into 2-inch chunks
1 pound petite Yukon gold potatoes, halved
1 package (10 ounces) frozen peas

Slow Cooker Directions

1. Cook and stir onion in 1½ teaspoons bacon fat in large skillet over medium heat until golden. Add to slow cooker.

2. Mix flour with salt and pepper in large bowl. Dredge lamb in flour mixture. Heat 1 tablespoon bacon fat in skillet over medium-high heat until hot. Add half of lamb to skillet; cook until browned on all sides. Add 1 tablespoon sugar; mix well to coat meat. Cook several minutes, until meat is caramelized. Add meat to slow cooker. Repeat with remaining lamb, using remaining 1 to 2 tablespoons bacon fat as needed and remaining 1 tablespoon sugar.

3. Add broth to skillet and boil over high heat, scraping sides and bottom of pan to loosen browned bits. Add tomato paste, garlic, thyme, rosemary and bay leaves. Stir to combine. Pour over meat mixture in slow cooker. Cover; cook on LOW 4 hours or on HIGH 2 hours.

4. Add carrots and potatoes. Cover; cook 3 to 4 hours more on LOW or 1½ to 2½ hours on HIGH or until vegetables and lamb are tender.

5. Add peas. Cook 30 minutes more. Remove and discard bay leaves before serving. *Makes 6 to 8 servings*

French Onion Soup

4 tablespoons butter
3 pounds yellow onions, sliced
1 tablespoon sugar
2 to 3 tablespoons dry white wine or water (optional)
8 cups beef broth
8 to 16 slices French bread
½ cup shredded Gruyère or Swiss cheese

Slow Cooker Directions

1. Melt butter in large skillet over medium to low heat. Add onions; cover and cook just until onions are limp and transparent, but not browned, about 10 minutes.

2. Remove cover. Sprinkle sugar over onions. Cook, stirring, until onions are caramelized, 8 to 10 minutes. Scrape onions and any browned bits into slow cooker. If desired, deglaze pan by adding wine to pan, returning to heat, bringing to a boil and scraping up any browned bits with a wooden spoon. Add to slow cooker with onions. Stir in broth. Cover; cook on LOW 8 hours or on HIGH 6 hours.

3. Preheat broiler. To serve, ladle soup into individual soup bowls; top with 1 or 2 slices bread and about 1 tablespoon cheese. Place under broiler until cheese is melted and bubbly.   *Makes 8 servings*

Variation: Substitute 2 cups dry white wine for beef broth.

Caribbean Sweet Potato & Bean Stew

Prep Time: *10 minutes* / **Cook Time:** *5 to 6 hours*

2 medium sweet potatoes (about 1 pound), peeled and cut into 1-inch cubes
2 cups frozen cut green beans
1 can (15 ounces) black beans, rinsed and drained
1 can (14½ ounces) vegetable broth
1 small onion, sliced
2 teaspoons Caribbean or Jamaican jerk seasoning
½ teaspoon dried thyme leaves
¼ teaspoon salt
¼ teaspoon ground cinnamon
⅓ cup slivered almonds, toasted*
   Hot pepper sauce (optional)

*To toast almonds, spread in single layer on baking sheet. Bake in preheated 350°F oven 8 to 10 minutes or until golden brown, stirring frequently.

Slow Cooker Directions

1. Combine sweet potatoes, beans, broth, onion, jerk seasoning, thyme, salt and cinnamon in slow cooker.

2. Cover; cook on LOW 5 to 6 hours or until vegetables are tender.

3. Adjust seasonings. Serve with almonds and hot pepper sauce, if desired.

Makes 4 servings

Caribbean Sweet Potato & Bean Stew

No-Chop Black Bean Soup

3 cans (15 ounces each) black beans, rinsed and drained
2 cups frozen chopped onions
1 package (12 ounces) frozen diced green bell peppers
2 cans (14½ ounces each) chicken broth
1 can (14½ ounces) diced tomatoes with peppers, celery and onions, undrained
1½ teaspoons ground cumin, divided
1 teaspoon minced garlic
¾ teaspoon salt
2 tablespoons olive oil

Slow Cooker Directions

1. Combine beans, onions, bell peppers, broth, tomatoes with juice, 1 teaspoon cumin and garlic in slow cooker.

2. Cover; cook on LOW 8 to 10 hours or on HIGH 5 hours.

3. Just before serving, stir in remaining ½ teaspoon cumin, salt and oil.

Makes 8 servings

Southwestern Chicken Chowder

1 can (15 ounces) VEG•ALL® Original Mixed Vegetables, drained
2 cups cubed cooked chicken
1 medium sweet red pepper, seeded & chopped
1½ cups whole milk
1 can (about 11 ounces) cream of chicken soup
1 cup mild green salsa, or thick and chunky salsa
1 tablespoon fresh lime juice
1 can (about 15 ounces) mild chili beans
1 tablespoon chopped fresh cilantro, optional

Combine all ingredients except cilantro in a 2- to 3-quart crock pot. Cook on low for 1 to 2 hours or until heated through.

Add cilantro and serve.

Makes 6 to 8 servings

No-Chop Black Bean Soup

Pasta Fagioli Soup

2 cans (14½ ounces each) beef broth
1 can (16 ounces) Great Northern beans, rinsed and drained
1 can (14½ ounces) diced tomatoes, undrained
2 medium zucchini, quartered lengthwise and sliced
1 tablespoon olive oil
1½ teaspoons minced garlic
½ teaspoon *each* dried basil leaves and dried oregano leaves
½ cup tubetti, ditilini or small shell pasta, uncooked
½ cup *each* garlic seasoned croutons and grated Romano cheese
3 tablespoons chopped fresh basil or Italian parsley (optional)

Slow Cooker Directions

1. Combine broth, beans, tomatoes with juice, zucchini, oil, garlic, dried basil and oregano in slow cooker; mix well. Cover; cook on LOW 3 to 4 hours.

2. Stir in pasta. Cover; continue cooking on LOW 1 hour or until pasta is tender.

3. Serve soup with croutons and cheese. Garnish with fresh basil, if desired.

Makes 5 to 6 servings

Simmered Split Pea Soup

3 cans (14½ ounces each) chicken broth
1 package (16 ounces) dry split peas
1 medium onion, diced
2 medium carrots, diced
1 teaspoon black pepper
½ teaspoon dried thyme leaves
1 bay leaf
8 slices bacon, crisp-cooked and crumbled, divided

Slow Cooker Directions

1. Place all ingredients and half of bacon in slow cooker. Cover; cook on LOW 6 to 8 hours or until vegetables are tender.

2. Remove bay leaf and adjust seasonings. Garnish with remaining bacon.

Makes 6 servings

Pasta Fagioli Soup

Middle Eastern Lamb and Bean Stew

2 tablespoons olive oil

1 lamb shank (1 to 1½ pounds)

4 cups chicken broth

5 cloves garlic, crushed

8 peppercorns

2 slices bacon, chopped

2 pounds boneless lamb stew meat

½ cup all-purpose flour

½ medium onion, chopped

2 cans (15 ounces each) cannellini beans, rinsed and drained

2 carrots, sliced

2 to 3 stalks celery, sliced diagonally into 1-inch slices

¼ cup cornstarch or arrowroot

¼ cup water

Salt and black pepper

Chopped fresh herbs (optional)

Slow Cooker Directions

1. Heat oil in large skillet over medium-high heat. Brown lamb shank on all sides. Place in slow cooker. Add chicken broth, garlic and peppercorns. Cover; cook on HIGH 2 hours.

2. Add bacon to same skillet. Cook until crisp. Coat stew meat with flour; shake off excess. Brown ½ stew meat on all sides; add to slow cooker. Brown remaining ½ stew meat and onion, adding additional oil, if needed. Add lamb mixture, beans, carrots and celery to slow cooker. Cover; cook on LOW an additional 6 hours.

3. Remove cover 30 minutes before serving. Remove lamb shank; discard. Let liquid stand 5 minutes to allow fat to rise. Skim off fat. Mix cornstarch and water until smooth; stir into slow cooker. Cook, uncovered, 30 minutes or until thickened. Season with salt and pepper. Sprinkle with chopped fresh herbs, if desired.   *Makes 4 to 6 servings*

Middle Eastern Lamb and Bean Stew

Chinese Chicken Stew

1 pound boneless skinless chicken thighs, cut into 1-inch pieces
1 teaspoon Chinese five-spice powder*
½ to ¾ teaspoon red pepper flakes
1 tablespoon peanut or vegetable oil
1 large onion, coarsely chopped
1 package (8 ounces) fresh mushrooms, sliced
2 cloves garlic, minced
1 can (about 14 ounces) chicken broth, divided
1 tablespoon cornstarch
1 large red bell pepper, cut into ¾-inch pieces
2 tablespoons soy sauce
2 large green onions, cut into ½-inch pieces
1 tablespoon sesame oil
3 cups hot cooked white rice (optional)
¼ cup coarsely chopped fresh cilantro (optional)

Chinese five-spice powder is a blend of cinnamon, cloves, fennel seed, anise and Szechuan peppercorns. It is available in most supermarkets and at Asian grocery stores.

Slow Cooker Directions

1. Toss chicken with five-spice powder and red pepper flakes in small bowl. Heat peanut oil in large skillet. Add onion and chicken; cook and stir about 5 minutes or until chicken is browned. Add mushrooms and garlic; cook and stir until chicken is no longer pink.

2. Combine ¼ cup broth and cornstarch in small bowl; set aside. Place cooked chicken mixture, remaining 1½ cups broth, bell pepper and soy sauce in slow cooker. Cover; cook on LOW 3½ hours or until peppers are tender.

3. Stir in cornstarch mixture, green onions and sesame oil. Cook 30 to 45 minutes or until juices have thickened. Ladle into soup bowls; scoop ½ cup rice into each bowl and sprinkle with cilantro, if desired.

Makes 6 servings (about 5 cups)

Southwest Bean Chili

1 can (16 ounces) tomato sauce
1 can (15 ounces) garbanzo beans, rinsed and drained
1 can (15 ounces) red kidney beans, rinsed and drained
1 can (15 ounces) black beans, rinsed and drained
1 can (14½ ounces) Mexican-style stewed tomatoes, undrained
1½ cups frozen corn
2 medium green bell peppers, chopped
1 cup chicken broth
3 tablespoons chili powder
4 cloves garlic, minced
1 tablespoon unsweetened cocoa powder
1 teaspoon ground cumin
½ teaspoon salt
   Hot cooked rice

Toppings
   Shredded cheese, sliced ripe olives, avocado and green onion slices
      (optional)

Slow Cooker Directions

1. Combine all ingredients except rice and toppings in slow cooker; stir until well blended. Cover; cook on LOW 6 to 6½ hours or until vegetables are tender.

2. Spoon rice into bowls; top with chili. Serve with toppings, if desired.

Makes 8 to 10 servings

SIDE DISHES

Peasant Potatoes

¼ cup (½ stick) unsalted butter
1 large onion, chopped
2 large cloves garlic, chopped
½ pound smoked beef sausage, cut into ¾-inch slices
1 teaspoon dried oregano leaves
6 medium potatoes, preferably Yukon Gold, cut into 1½- to 2-inch pieces
   Salt and black pepper
2 cups sliced Savoy or other cabbage
1 cup diced or sliced roasted red bell pepper
½ cup shaved fresh Parmesan cheese

Slow Cooker Directions

1. Melt butter in large skillet over medium heat. Add onion and garlic. Cook and stir 5 minutes or until onion is transparent. Stir in sausage and oregano; cook 5 minutes. Stir in potatoes, salt and black pepper until well blended. Transfer mixture to slow cooker.

2. Cover; cook on LOW 6 to 8 hours or on HIGH 3 to 4 hours, stirring every hour if possible. During last 30 minutes of cooking, add cabbage and bell pepper.

3. Sprinkle with Parmesan cheese just before serving.   *Makes 6 servings*

Winter Squash and Apples

1 **butternut squash (about 2 pounds), peeled, seeded and cut into 2-inch pieces**
2 **apples, cored and cut into slices**
1 **medium onion, quartered and sliced**
   Salt and black pepper
1½ **tablespoons butter**

Slow Cooker Directions

1. Place squash in slow cooker. Add apples and onion. Sprinkle with salt and black pepper; stir well. Cover; cook on LOW 6 to 7 hours.

2. Before serving, stir in butter and season with additional salt and pepper, if desired.   *Makes 4 to 6 servings*

New England Baked Beans

4 **slices uncooked bacon, chopped**
3 **cans (15 ounces each) Great Northern beans, rinsed and drained**
¾ **cup water**
1 **small onion, chopped**
⅓ **cup canned diced tomatoes, well drained**
3 **tablespoons *each* packed light brown sugar, maple syrup and unsulphured molasses**
2 **cloves garlic, minced**
½ **teaspoon *each* salt and dry mustard**
⅛ **teaspoon black pepper**
1 **bay leaf**

Slow Cooker Directions

1. Cook bacon in large skillet until almost cooked but not crispy. Drain on paper towels.

2. Combine bacon and remaining ingredients in slow cooker. Cover; cook on LOW 6 to 8 hours or until onion is tender and mixture is thickened. Remove bay leaf before serving.   *Makes 4 to 6 servings*

Winter Squash and Apples

Spanish Paella-Style Rice

Prep Time: *10 minutes* / **Cook Time:** *4½ hours*

2 cans (14½ ounces each) chicken broth
1½ cups converted long grain rice, uncooked (not quick cooking or
    instant rice)
1 small red bell pepper, diced
⅓ cup dry white wine or water
½ teaspoon powdered saffron *or* ½ teaspoon turmeric
⅛ teaspoon red pepper flakes
½ cup frozen peas, thawed
    Salt

Slow Cooker Directions

1. Combine broth, rice, bell pepper, wine, saffron and red pepper flakes in slow cooker; mix well.

2. Cover; cook on LOW 4 hours or until liquid is absorbed.

3. Stir in peas. Cover; cook on LOW 15 to 30 minutes longer or until peas are hot. Season with salt.   *Makes 6 servings*

Variations: Add ½ cup cooked chicken or ham cubes, shrimp or quartered marinated artichokes, drained, at the same time the peas are added.

COOK'S TIP

Paella is a Spanish dish of saffron-flavored
rice combined with a variety of meats,
seafood and vegetables. Paella is traditionally
served in a wide, shallow dish.

Spanish Paella-Style Rice

Eggplant Italiano

Prep Time: *10 minutes* / **Cook Time:** *3½ to 6 hours*

1¼ pounds eggplant, cut into 1-inch cubes
2 medium onions, thinly sliced
2 ribs celery, cut into 1-inch pieces
1 can (16 ounces) diced tomatoes, undrained
3 tablespoons tomato sauce
1 tablespoon olive oil
½ cup pitted ripe olives, cut in half
2 tablespoons balsamic vinegar
1 tablespoon sugar
1 tablespoon capers, drained
1 teaspoon dried oregano or basil leaves
Salt and black pepper to taste
Fresh basil leaves, leaf lettuce and red jalapeño pepper* (optional)

Jalapeño peppers can sting and irritate the skin; wear rubber gloves when handling peppers and do not touch eyes. Wash hands after handling.

Slow Cooker Directions

1. Combine eggplant, onions, celery, tomatoes with juice, tomato sauce and oil in slow cooker. Cover; cook on LOW 3½ to 4 hours or until eggplant is tender.

2. Stir in olives, vinegar, sugar, capers and oregano. Season with salt and black pepper. Cover; cook 45 minutes to 1 hour or until heated through. Garnish with basil, lettuce and jalapeño pepper, if desired.   *Makes 6 servings*

No-Fuss Macaroni & Cheese

Prep Time: *10 minutes* / **Cook Time:** *2 to 3 hours*

2 cups (about 8 ounces) uncooked elbow macaroni
4 ounces pasteurized processed cheese, cubed
1 cup (4 ounces) shredded mild Cheddar cheese
½ teaspoon salt
⅛ teaspoon black pepper
1½ cups milk

Slow Cooker Directions

Combine macaroni, cheeses, salt and pepper in slow cooker. Pour milk over top. Cover; cook on LOW 2 to 3 hours, stirring after 20 to 30 minutes.

Makes 6 to 8 servings

Variation: Stir in desired vegetable.

COOK'S TIP

As with all macaroni and cheese dishes, as it sits, the cheese sauce thickens and begins to dry out. If it dries out, stir in a little extra milk and heat through. Do not cook longer than 4 hours.

Orange-Spiced Sweet Potatoes

 2 pounds sweet potatoes, peeled and diced
 1/2 cup (1 stick) butter, cut into small pieces
 1/2 cup packed dark brown sugar
 1 teaspoon ground cinnamon
 1 teaspoon vanilla
 1/2 teaspoon ground nutmeg
 1/2 teaspoon orange zest
    Juice of 1 medium orange
 1/4 teaspoon salt
    Chopped, toasted pecans (optional)

Slow Cooker Directions
Place all ingredients in slow cooker, except pecans. Cover; cook on LOW
4 hours or on HIGH 2 hours or until potatoes are tender. Sprinkle with pecans
before serving, if desired. *Makes 8 (1/2-cup) servings*

Variation: Mash potatoes with a hand masher or electric mixer; add 1/4 cup
milk or cream for a moister consistency. Sprinkle with a cinnamon-sugar
mixture.

Scalloped Tomatoes & Corn

Prep Time: *7 minutes* / **Cook Time:** *4 to 6 hours*

 1 can (15 ounces) cream-style corn
 1 can (14 1/2 ounces) diced tomatoes, undrained
 3/4 cup saltine cracker crumbs
 1 egg, lightly beaten
 2 teaspoons sugar
 3/4 teaspoon black pepper

Slow Cooker Directions
Combine all ingredients in slow cooker; mix well. Cover; cook on LOW 4 to
6 hours. *Makes 4 to 6 servings*

Orange-Spiced Sweet Potatoes

Skinny Corn Bread

1 1/4 cups all-purpose flour

3/4 cup yellow cornmeal

1/4 cup sugar

1 teaspoon baking powder

1 teaspoon baking soda

1 teaspoon seasoned salt

1 cup nonfat buttermilk

1/4 cup cholesterol-free egg substitute

1/4 cup canola oil

Slow Cooker Directions

1. Preheat slow cooker on HIGH.

2. Sift together flour, cornmeal, sugar, baking powder, baking soda and seasoned salt in large bowl. Make well in center of dry mixture. Pour in buttermilk, egg substitute and oil. Mix in dry ingredients just until moistened. Pour mixture into greased 2-quart soufflé dish or 2-pound coffee can.

3. Cover with lid or foil. Place on rack or metal trivet in preheated slow cooker. Cover; cook on LOW 3 to 4 hours or on HIGH 30 minutes to 2 hours or until edges are golden and knife inserted into center comes out clean.

Makes 8 servings

Note: You may wish to cook the corn bread with slow cooker lid slightly ajar to allow any condensation to evaporate.

Sunshine Squash

1 butternut squash (about 2 pounds), peeled, seeded and diced
1 can (about 15 ounces) kernel corn, drained
1 can (14½ ounces) tomatoes, undrained
1 medium onion, coarsely chopped
1 green bell pepper, cut into 1-inch pieces
½ cup chicken broth
1 canned green chili, coarsely chopped
1 clove garlic, minced
½ teaspoon salt
¼ teaspoon black pepper
1 tablespoon plus 1½ teaspoons tomato paste

Slow Cooker Directions

1. Combine all ingredients except tomato paste in slow cooker. Cover; cook on LOW 6 hours or until squash is tender.

2. Remove about ¼ cup cooking liquid and blend with tomato paste. Stir into slow cooker. Cook 30 minutes or until mixture is slightly thickened and heated through.   *Makes 6 to 8 servings*

Pesto Rice and Beans

1 can (15 ounces) Great Northern beans, rinsed and drained
1 can (14 ounces) chicken broth
¾ cup uncooked long-grain white rice
1½ cups frozen cut green beans, thawed and drained
½ cup prepared pesto

Slow Cooker Directions

1. Combine Great Northern beans, broth and rice in slow cooker. Cover; cook on LOW 2 hours.

2. Stir in green beans; cover and cook 1 hour or until rice and beans are tender. Turn off slow cooker; remove insert to heatproof surface. Stir in pesto. Let stand, covered, 5 minutes or until cheese is melted. Serve immediately.

Makes 8 servings

South-of-the-Border
Macaroni & Cheese

5 cups cooked rotini pasta

2 cups (8 ounces) cubed American cheese

1 can (12 ounces) evaporated milk

1 cup (4 ounces) cubed sharp Cheddar cheese

1 can (4 ounces) diced green chilies, drained

2 teaspoons chili powder

2 medium tomatoes, seeded and chopped

5 green onions, sliced

Slow Cooker Directions

1. Combine all ingredients, except tomatoes and onions in slow cooker; mix well. Cover; cook on HIGH 2 hours, stirring twice.

2. Stir in tomatoes and onions; continue cooking until hot.

Makes 4 servings

Blue Cheese Potatoes

2 pounds red potatoes, peeled and cut into ½-inch pieces

1¼ cups chopped green onions, divided

2 tablespoons olive oil, divided

1 teaspoon dried basil leaves

½ teaspoon salt

¼ teaspoon black pepper

2 ounces crumbled blue cheese

Slow Cooker Directions

1. Layer potatoes, 1 cup onions, 1 tablespoon oil, basil, salt and pepper in slow cooker. Cover; cook on LOW 7 hours or on HIGH 4 hours.

2. Gently stir in cheese and remaining 1 tablespoon oil. If slow cooker is on LOW, turn to HIGH; cook additional 5 minutes to allow flavors to blend. Transfer potatoes to serving platter and top with remaining ¼ cup onions.

Makes 5 servings

South-of-the-Border Macaroni & Cheese

Rustic Cheddar Mashed Potatoes

   2 pounds russet potatoes, peeled and diced
   1 cup water
   ⅓ cup butter, cut into small pieces
   ½ to ¾ cup milk
1¼ teaspoons salt
   ½ teaspoon black pepper
   ½ cup finely chopped green onions
   2 to 3 ounces shredded Cheddar cheese

Slow Cooker Directions

1. Combine potatoes and water in slow cooker; dot with butter. Cover; cook on LOW 6 hours or on HIGH 3 hours or until potatoes are tender.

2. Whip potatoes with electric mixer at medium speed until well blended. Add milk, salt and pepper; whip until well blended. Stir in green onions and cheese, cover tightly; let stand 15 minutes to allow flavors to blend and cheese to melt. *Makes 8 servings*

Easy Dirty Rice

   ½ pound bulk Italian sausage
   2 cups water
   1 cup uncooked long grain rice
   1 large onion, finely chopped
   1 large green bell pepper, finely chopped
   ½ cup finely chopped celery
1½ teaspoons salt
   ½ teaspoon ground red pepper
   ½ cup chopped fresh parsley

Slow Cooker Directions

1. Cook sausage in skillet, stirring to break up meat, until no longer pink. Place cooked sausage into slow cooker.

2. Stir in all remaining ingredients except parsley. Cover; cook on LOW 2 hours or until rice is tender. Stir in parsley. *Makes 4 servings*

Add even more great recipes to your collection!

FREE MAGAZINE

as our way of saying

thank you

for your purchase!

Just send in this card to register and we'll send you the next issue of EASY HOME COOKING Magazine FREE!

- More than 50 mouthwatering recipes featuring your favorite brand name foods.
- Beautiful color photos of finished recipes, plus helpful Cook's Notes and easy-to-follow cooking instructions.

Name

Address

City/State/ZIP

Canadian residents, please enclose $1.50 U.S. funds) for postage. This offer is not available outside North America. Please allow 4-6 weeks for delivery of first issue.

S69DGD

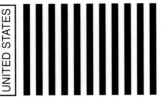

BUSINESS REPLY MAIL

FIRST-CLASS MAIL PERMIT NO. 24 MT. MORRIS, IL

POSTAGE WILL BE PAID BY ADDRESSEE

EASY HOME COOKING
PO BOX 520
MT MORRIS IL 61054-7451

Rustic Cheddar Mashed Potatoes

Cheesy Broccoli Casserole

Prep Time: *5 to 10 minutes* / **Cook Time:** *5½ to 7 hours*

2 packages (10 ounces each) frozen chopped broccoli, thawed
1 can (10¾ ounces) condensed cream of potato soup, undiluted
1¼ cups shredded sharp Cheddar cheese, divided
¼ cup minced onions
1 teaspoon hot pepper sauce
1 cup crushed saltine crackers or potato chips

Slow Cooker Directions

1. Lightly grease slow cooker. Combine broccoli, soup, 1 cup cheese, onions and hot pepper sauce in slow cooker; mix thoroughly.

2. Cover; cook on LOW 5 to 6 hours or on HIGH 2½ to 3 hours.

3. Uncover; sprinkle top with crackers and remaining ¼ cup cheese. Cook, uncovered, on LOW 30 to 60 minutes or until cheese melts.

Makes 4 to 6 servings

Variation: If desired, casserole can be spooned into a baking dish and garnished with additional cheese and crackers; bake in a preheated 400°F oven for 5 to 10 minutes.

Parmesan Potato Wedges

2 pounds red potatoes, cut into ½-inch wedges
¼ cup finely chopped yellow onion
2 tablespoons butter, cut into ⅛-inch pieces
1½ teaspoons dried oregano leaves
½ teaspoon salt
Black pepper to taste
¼ cup (1 ounce) grated Parmesan cheese

Slow Cooker Directions

Layer potatoes, onion, butter, oregano, salt and pepper in slow cooker. Cover; cook on HIGH 4 hours. Transfer potatoes to serving platter and sprinkle with cheese.

Makes 6 servings

Cheesy Broccoli Casserole

Mediterranean Red Potatoes

3 medium red potatoes, cut in half lengthwise, then crosswise into pieces
²/₃ cup fresh or frozen pearl onions
    Nonstick garlic-flavored cooking spray
¾ teaspoon dried Italian seasoning
¼ teaspoon black pepper
1 small tomato, seeded and chopped
2 ounces (½ cup) feta cheese, crumbled
2 tablespoons chopped black olives

Slow Cooker Directions

1. Place potatoes and onions in 1½-quart soufflé dish. Spray potatoes and onions with cooking spray; toss to coat. Add Italian seasoning and pepper; mix well. Cover dish tightly with foil.

2. Tear off 3 (18×3-inch) strips of heavy-duty aluminum foil. Cross strips to resemble wheel spokes. Place soufflé dish in center of strips. Pull foil strips up and over dish; place dish into slow cooker.

3. Pour hot water into slow cooker to about 1½ inches from top of soufflé dish. Cover; cook on LOW 7 to 8 hours.

4. Use foil handles to lift dish out of slow cooker. Stir tomato, cheese and olives into potato mixture. *Makes 4 servings*

Mediterranean Red Potatoes

Southwestern Corn and Beans

Prep Time: *15 minutes* / **Cook Time:** *7 to 8 hours*

1 tablespoon olive oil
1 large onion, diced
1 or 2 jalapeño peppers,* diced
1 clove garlic, minced
2 cans (15 ounces each) light red kidney beans, rinsed and drained
1 bag (16 ounces) frozen corn
1 can (14½ ounces) diced tomatoes, undrained
1 green bell pepper, cut into 1-inch pieces
2 teaspoons medium-hot chili powder
¾ teaspoon salt
½ teaspoon ground cumin
½ teaspoon black pepper
1 carton (8 ounces) plain yogurt (optional)
  Sliced black olives (optional)

Jalapeño peppers can sting and irritate the skin; wear rubber gloves when handling peppers and do not touch eyes. Wash hands after handling.

Slow Cooker Directions

1. Heat oil in medium skillet over medium heat. Add onion, jalapeño pepper and garlic; cook and stir 5 minutes. Add onion mixture, kidney beans, corn, tomatoes with juice, bell pepper, chili powder, salt, cumin and black pepper to slow cooker.

2. Cover; cook on LOW 7 to 8 hours.

3. Spoon corn and beans into bowls. Serve with yogurt and black olives, if desired. *Makes 6 servings*

Tip: For a party, spoon this colorful vegetarian dish into hollowed-out bread bowls.

Southwestern Corn and Beans

Swiss Cheese Scalloped Potatoes

2 pounds baking potatoes, peeled and thinly sliced
½ cup finely chopped yellow onion
¼ teaspoon salt
¼ teaspoon ground nutmeg
2 tablespoons butter, cut into small pieces
½ cup milk
2 tablespoons all-purpose flour
3 ounces Swiss cheese slices, torn into small pieces
¼ cup finely chopped green onions (optional)

Slow Cooker Directions

1. Layer half of potatoes, ¼ cup yellow onion, ⅛ teaspoon salt, ⅛ teaspoon nutmeg and 1 tablespoon butter in slow cooker. Repeat layers. Cover; cook on LOW 7 hours or on HIGH 4 hours. Remove potatoes with slotted spoon to serving dish and keep warm.

2. Blend milk and flour in small bowl until smooth. Stir mixture into slow cooker. Add cheese; stir to combine. If slow cooker is on LOW, turn to HIGH. Cover; cook until slightly thickened, about 10 minutes. Stir. Pour cheese mixture over potatoes and serve. Garnish with chopped green onions, if desired.   *Makes 5 to 6 servings*

Swiss Cheese Scalloped Potatoes

Risotto-Style Peppered Rice

1 cup uncooked converted long grain rice
1 cup chopped onion
1 medium green bell pepper, chopped
1 medium red bell pepper, chopped
½ teaspoon ground turmeric
⅛ teaspoon ground red pepper (optional)
1 can (14½ ounces) chicken broth
4 ounces Monterey Jack cheese with jalapeño peppers, cubed
½ cup milk
¼ cup (½ stick) butter, cubed
1 teaspoon salt

Slow Cooker Directions

1. Place rice, onion, bell peppers, turmeric and ground red pepper, if desired, into slow cooker. Stir in broth.

2. Cover; cook on LOW 4 to 5 hours or until rice is done.

3. Stir in cheese, milk, butter and salt; fluff rice with fork. Cover; cook on LOW 5 minutes or until cheese melts. *Makes 4 to 6 servings*

Busy-Day Rice

2 cups water
1 cup converted white rice
2 tablespoons butter
1 tablespoon *each* dried minced onion and dried parsley flakes
2 teaspoons chicken bouillon granules
   Dash ground red pepper (optional)

Slow Cooker Directions

Combine all ingredients in slow cooker; mix well. Cover; cook on HIGH 2 hours or until rice is tender. *Makes 4 servings*

Variation: During the last 30 minutes of cooking, add ½ cup green peas, tiny broccoli florets or diced carrots.

Risotto-Style Peppered Rice

Scalloped Potatoes and Parsnips

¼ cup (½ stick) plus 2 tablespoons unsalted butter
3 tablespoons all-purpose flour
1¾ cups heavy cream
2 teaspoons dry mustard
1½ teaspoons salt
1 teaspoon dried thyme leaves
½ teaspoon black pepper
2 baking potatoes, cut in half lengthwise, then in ¼-inch slices crosswise
2 parsnips, cut into ¼-inch slices
1 onion, chopped
2 cups (8 ounces) shredded sharp Cheddar cheese

Slow Cooker Directions

1. Melt butter in medium saucepan over medium-high heat. Add flour and whisk constantly 3 to 5 minutes. Slowly whisk in cream, mustard, salt, thyme and pepper. Stir until smooth.

2. Place potatoes, parsnips and onion in slow cooker. Add cream sauce.

3. Cover; cook on LOW 7 hours or on HIGH 3½ hours or until potatoes are tender. Stir in cheese. Cover until cheese melts.   *Makes 4 to 6 servings*

Scalloped Potatoes and Parsnips

Delicious Parsnip Casserole

Prep Time: *30 minutes* / **Cook Time:** *4 to 5 hours*

2 pounds parsnips, peeled and sliced
1 cup (4 ounces) shredded sharp Cheddar cheese
⅔ cup evaporated milk
¼ cup saltine cracker crumbs
6 slices bacon, crisp-cooked and crumbled
1 egg, well beaten
1½ teaspoons prepared horseradish
1 teaspoon salt
¼ teaspoon black pepper
Butter

Slow Cooker Directions

1. Cook parsnips in boiling water about 15 minutes or until tender; drain well. Mash with potato masher until creamy. Add all remaining ingredients except butter; blend well.

2. Spoon mixture into buttered slow cooker. Cover; cook on LOW 4 to 5 hours.

Makes 4 to 6 servings

Slow Roasted Potatoes

16 small new potatoes
3 tablespoons butter, cut into ⅛-inch pieces
1 teaspoon paprika
½ teaspoon salt
¼ teaspoon garlic powder
Black pepper to taste

Slow Cooker Directions

1. Combine all ingredients in slow cooker; mix well. Cover; cook on LOW 7 hours or on HIGH 4 hours.

2. Remove potatoes with slotted spoon to serving dish; cover to keep warm. Add 1 to 2 tablespoons water to drippings and stir until well blended. Pour mixture over potatoes.

Makes 3 to 4 servings

Simmered Red Beans with Rice

2 cans (15 ounces each) red beans, rinsed and drained
1 can (14½ ounces) diced tomatoes, undrained
½ cup chopped celery
½ cup chopped green onions with tops
½ cup chopped green bell pepper
2 cloves garlic, minced
1 to 2 teaspoons hot pepper sauce
1 teaspoon Worcestershire sauce
1 bay leaf
   Hot cooked rice

Slow Cooker Directions

1. Combine all ingredients except rice in slow cooker. Cover; cook on LOW 4 to 6 hours or on HIGH 2 to 3 hours.

2. Slightly mash mixture in slow cooker with potato masher to thicken. Continue to cook on LOW 30 to 60 minutes. Serve over rice.

Makes 6 (1-cup) servings

Rustic Garlic Mashed Potatoes

2 pounds baking potatoes, unpeeled and cut into ½-inch cubes
¼ cup water
2 tablespoons butter, cut into ⅛-inch pieces
1¼ teaspoons salt
½ teaspoon garlic powder
¼ teaspoon black pepper
1 cup milk

Slow Cooker Directions

Place all ingredients except milk in slow cooker; toss to combine. Cover; cook on LOW 7 hours or on HIGH 4 hours. Add milk to potatoes. Mash potatoes with potato masher or electric mixer until smooth.

Makes 5 servings

MAIN ENTRÉES

Honey-Mustard Chicken Wings

Prep Time: *20 minutes* / **Cook Time:** *4 to 5 hours*

3 pounds chicken wings
1 teaspoon salt
1 teaspoon black pepper
½ cup honey
½ cup barbecue sauce
2 tablespoons spicy brown mustard
1 clove garlic, minced
3 to 4 thin lemon slices

Slow Cooker Directions

1. Rinse chicken and pat dry. Cut off wing tips; discard. Cut each wing at joint to make two pieces. Sprinkle salt and pepper on both sides of chicken. Place wing pieces on broiler rack. Broil 4 to 5 inches from heat about 10 minutes, turning halfway through cooking time. Place broiled chicken wings in slow cooker.

2. Combine honey, barbecue sauce, mustard and garlic in small bowl; mix well. Pour sauce over chicken wings. Top with lemon slices. Cover; cook on LOW 4 to 5 hours.

3. Remove and discard lemon slices. Serve wings with sauce.

Makes about 24 wings

Pork Roast Landaise

2 tablespoons olive oil
2½ pounds boneless center cut pork loin roast
Salt and black pepper
1 medium onion, diced
2 large cloves garlic, minced
2 teaspoons dried thyme leaves
2 cups chicken broth or stock, divided
2 tablespoons cornstarch or arrowroot
¼ cup sugar
¼ cup red wine vinegar
½ cup port or sherry wine
2 parsnips, cut into ¾-inch-thick slices
3 pears, cored and cut into ¾-inch-thick slices
1½ cups pitted prunes

Slow Cooker Directions

1. Heat olive oil in large saucepan over medium-high heat. Season pork roast with salt and pepper; brown in saucepan on all sides. Transfer browned roast to slow cooker.

2. Blend ¼ cup chicken broth and cornstarch in small bowl until smooth; set aside.

3. Add onion and garlic to saucepan; cook and stir over medium heat for 2 to 3 minutes. Stir in thyme. Add onion mixture to slow cooker.

4. In same saucepan combine sugar and vinegar. Cook over medium heat, stirring constantly, until mixture becomes syrupy. Add port; cook 1 minute more. Add remaining 1¾ cups chicken broth. Stir cornstarch mixture; whisk into broth mixture. Cook and stir until smooth and slightly thickened. Pour into slow cooker.

5. Cover; cook on LOW 8 hours or on HIGH 4 hours. During last 30 minutes of cooking, add parsnips, pears and prunes.   *Makes 4 to 6 servings*

Serving Suggestion: Serve over rice or mashed potatoes or with French bread to dunk in the gravy.

Pork Roast Landaise

Slow Cooker Brisket of Beef

1 whole well-trimmed beef brisket (about 5 pounds)
2 teaspoons bottled minced garlic
½ teaspoon black pepper
2 large onions, cut into ¼-inch slices and separated into rings
1 bottle (12 ounces) chili sauce
12 ounces beef broth, dark ale or water
2 tablespoons Worcestershire sauce
1 tablespoon packed brown sugar

Slow Cooker Directions

1. Place brisket, fat side down, in slow cooker. Spread garlic evenly over brisket; sprinkle with pepper. Arrange onions over brisket. Combine chili sauce, broth, Worcestershire sauce and brown sugar; pour over brisket and onions. Cover; cook on LOW 8 hours.

2. Turn brisket over; stir onions into sauce and spoon over brisket. Add vegetables, if desired. Cover; cook until fork-tender. Transfer brisket to cutting board. Tent with foil; let stand 10 minutes.*

3. Stir juices in slow cooker. Spoon off and discard fat from juices. (Juices may be thinned to desired consistency with water or thickened by simmering, uncovered, in saucepan.) Carve brisket across grain into thin slices. Spoon juices over brisket.   *Makes 10 to 12 servings*

*At this point, brisket may be covered and refrigerated up to one day before serving. To reheat brisket, cut diagonally into thin slices. Place brisket slices and juice in large skillet. Cover; cook over medium-low heat until heated through.

Variation: Stir diced red boiling potatoes, cut carrots, sliced parsnips or turnips into juices during last hour of cooking time.

Slow Cooker Brisket of Beef

Italian-Style Pot Roast

Prep Time: *15 minutes* / **Cook Time:** *8 to 9 hours*

2 teaspoons minced garlic

1 teaspoon salt

1 teaspoon dried basil leaves

1 teaspoon dried oregano leaves

¼ teaspoon red pepper flakes

1 boneless beef bottom round rump or chuck shoulder roast (about 2½ to 3 pounds)

1 large onion, quartered and thinly sliced

1½ cups prepared tomato-basil or marinara pasta sauce

2 cans (16 ounces each) Great Northern or cannellini beans, rinsed and drained

¼ cup shredded fresh basil or chopped Italian parsley (optional)

Slow Cooker Directions

1. Combine garlic, salt, basil, oregano and red pepper flakes in small bowl; rub over roast.

2. Place half of onion slices into slow cooker. Cut roast in half to fit into slow cooker. Place one half of roast over onion slices; top with remaining onion slices and other half of roast. Pour pasta sauce over roast. Cover; cook on LOW 8 to 9 hours or until roast is fork tender.

3. Remove roast from cooking liquid; tent with foil. Let liquid in slow cooker stand 5 minutes to allow fat to rise. Skim off fat.

4. Stir beans into liquid. Cover; cook on HIGH 10 to 15 minutes or until beans are hot. Carve roast across grain into thin slices. Serve with bean mixture and garnish with fresh basil, if desired. *Makes 6 to 8 servings*

Italian-Style Pot Roast

Meatballs in Burgundy Sauce

60 frozen prepared fully-cooked meatballs
3 cups chopped onions
1½ cups water
1 cup red wine
2 packages (about 1 ounce each) beef gravy mix
¼ cup ketchup
1 tablespoon dried oregano leaves
1 package (8 ounces) curly noodles

Slow Cooker Directions

1. Combine meatballs, onions, water, wine, gravy mix, ketchup and oregano in slow cooker; stir to blend.

2. Cover; cook on HIGH 5 hours.

3. Meanwhile cook noodles according to package directions. Serve meatballs over noodles. *Makes 6 to 8 servings*

Sweet and Spicy Sausage Rounds

1 pound Kielbasa sausage, cut into ¼-inch rounds
⅔ cup blackberry jam
⅓ cup steak sauce
1 tablespoon prepared mustard
½ teaspoon ground allspice
Hot cooked rice
Chopped green onions

Slow Cooker Directions

1. Place all ingredients in slow cooker; toss to coat completely. Cook on HIGH 3 hours or until thickly glazed.

2. Serve over rice tossed with chopped green onions. *Makes 3 cups*

Meatballs in Burgundy Sauce

Greek-Style Chicken

Prep Time: *15 minutes* / **Cook Time:** *5 to 6 hours*

6 boneless skinless chicken thighs
$\frac{1}{2}$ teaspoon salt
$\frac{1}{2}$ teaspoon black pepper
1 tablespoon olive oil
$\frac{1}{2}$ cup chicken broth
1 lemon, thinly sliced
$\frac{1}{4}$ cup pitted kalamata olives
1 clove garlic, minced
$\frac{1}{2}$ teaspoon dried oregano leaves
    Hot cooked orzo or rice

Slow Cooker Directions

1. Remove visible fat from chicken; sprinkle chicken thighs with salt and pepper. Heat oil in large skillet over medium-high heat. Brown chicken on all sides. Place in slow cooker.

2. Add broth, lemon, olives, garlic and oregano to slow cooker.

3. Cover; cook on LOW 5 to 6 hours or until chicken is tender. Serve with orzo.   *Makes 4 to 6 servings*

Greek-Style Chicken

Ale'd Pork and Sauerkraut

1 jar (32 ounces) sauerkraut, undrained
1 tablespoon plus 1½ teaspoons sugar
1 can (12 ounces) dark beer or ale
3½ pounds boneless pork shoulder or pork butt roast
½ teaspoon salt
¼ teaspoon *each* garlic powder and black pepper
Paprika

Slow Cooker Directions

1. Place sauerkraut in slow cooker. Sprinkle sugar evenly over sauerkraut; pour beer over all. Place pork, fat side up, on top of sauerkraut mixture; sprinkle evenly with remaining ingredients.

2. Cover; cook on HIGH 6 hours.

3. Remove pork to serving platter; arrange sauerkraut around pork. Spoon cooking liquid over sauerkraut. *Makes 6 to 8 servings*

Lemon-Thyme Beef with Beans

1 beef chuck roast (about 3 pounds), trimmed and cut into 2-inch pieces
2 cans (15 ounces each) white or pinto beans, rinsed and drained
1 can (15 ounces) red kidney beans, rinsed and drained
1 cup beef broth
1 medium onion, chopped
2 cloves garlic, minced
1 teaspoon *each* salt, grated lemon peel, dried thyme leaves and black pepper
Chopped fresh parsley (optional)

Slow Cooker Directions

1. Place all ingredients, except parsley, in slow cooker. Cover; cook on LOW 8 to 9 hours or until beef is tender.

2. Adjust seasonings before serving, if desired. Arrange beef on top of beans. Garnish with parsley, if desired. *Makes 6 to 8 servings*

Ale'd Pork and Sauerkraut

Ham Meat Loaf with Horseradish Sauce

Prep Time: *20 minutes* / **Cook Time:** *4 to 4½ hours*

1½ pounds meat loaf mix* or ground beef
½ pound cooked ham, finely chopped
1 cup plain dry bread crumbs
1 cup finely chopped onion
2 eggs, lightly beaten
½ cup chili sauce or ketchup
1 teaspoon plus ⅛ teaspoon salt, divided
½ teaspoon caraway seeds
¼ teaspoon black pepper
½ cup sour cream
3 tablespoons thinly sliced green onions
1 tablespoon prepared horseradish
1 tablespoon spicy brown or coarse-grained mustard

Meat loaf mix is a combination of ground beef, pork and veal; see your meat retailer or make your own with 1 pound lean ground beef, ¼ pound ground pork and ¼ pound ground veal.

Slow Cooker Directions

1. Combine meat loaf mix, ham, bread crumbs, onion, eggs, chili sauce, 1 teaspoon salt, caraway seeds and pepper in large bowl; mix well. Shape meat mixture into 7-inch round loaf.

2. Prepare foil handles** for slow cooker. Place meat loaf on top of foil strips. Using strips, place meat loaf into slow cooker. Cover; cook on LOW 4 to 4½ hours or until meat thermometer inserted into center of meat loaf reads 165°F. Use foil strips to remove meat loaf from slow cooker. Let stand 5 minutes.

3. Meanwhile, combine sour cream, green onions, horseradish, mustard and remaining ⅛ teaspoon salt in small bowl; mix well. Cut meat loaf into wedges; serve with horseradish sauce.   *Makes 8 servings*

**Tear off three 18×2-inch strips of heavy foil or use regular foil folded to double thickness. Crisscross foil strips in spoke design.*

Beef with Apples and Sweet Potatoes

Prep Time: *20 minutes /* **Cook Time:** *8 to 9 hours*

1 boneless beef chuck shoulder roast (2 pounds), trimmed of fat and cut
   into 2-inch pieces
1 can (40 ounces) sweet potatoes, drained
2 small onions, sliced
2 apples, cored and sliced
½ cup beef broth
2 cloves garlic, minced
1 teaspoon salt
1 teaspoon dried thyme leaves, divided
¾ teaspoon black pepper, divided
1 tablespoon cornstarch
¼ teaspoon ground cinnamon
2 tablespoons cold water

Slow Cooker Directions

1. Place beef, sweet potatoes, onions, apples, broth, garlic, salt, ½ teaspoon
thyme and ½ teaspoon pepper in slow cooker. Cover; cook on LOW 8 to
9 hours.

2. Transfer beef, sweet potatoes and apples to platter; keep warm. Let liquid
stand 5 minutes to allow fat to rise. Skim off fat.

3. Combine cornstarch, remaining ½ teaspoon thyme, ¼ teaspoon pepper,
cinnamon and water; stir into cooking liquid. Cook 15 minutes or until juices
are thickened. Serve sauce with beef, sweet potatoes and apples.

Makes 6 servings

Saucy Tropical Turkey

Prep Time: *15 minutes* / **Cook Time:** *6½ to 7½ hours*

3 to 4 turkey thighs, skin removed (about 2½ pounds)
2 tablespoons vegetable oil
1 small onion, halved and sliced
1 can (20 ounces) pineapple chunks, drained
1 red bell pepper, cubed
⅔ cup apricot preserves
3 tablespoons soy sauce
1 teaspoon grated lemon peel
1 teaspoon ground ginger
¼ cup cold water
2 tablespoons cornstarch
    Hot cooked rice

Slow Cooker Directions

1. Rinse turkey and pat dry. Heat oil in large skillet; brown turkey on all sides. Place onion in slow cooker. Transfer turkey to slow cooker; top with pineapple and bell pepper.

2. Combine preserves, soy sauce, lemon peel and ginger in small bowl; mix well. Spoon over turkey. Cover; cook on LOW 6 to 7 hours.

3. Remove turkey from slow cooker; keep warm. Blend water and cornstarch until smooth; stir into slow cooker. Cook on HIGH 15 minutes or until sauce is slightly thickened. Adjust seasonings. Return turkey to slow cooker; cook until hot. Serve with rice.   *Makes 6 servings*

Saucy Tropical Turkey

Italian-Style Sausage with Rice

1 pound mild Italian sausage links, cut into 1-inch pieces
1 can (15 ounces) pinto beans, rinsed and drained
1 cup pasta sauce
1 green bell pepper, cut into strips
1 small onion, halved and sliced
$\frac{1}{2}$ teaspoon salt
$\frac{1}{4}$ teaspoon black pepper
   Hot cooked rice

Slow Cooker Directions

1. Brown sausage in large skillet over medium heat. Pour off drippings. Place all ingredients except rice into slow cooker. Cover; cook on LOW 4 to 6 hours.

2. Serve with rice.   *Makes 4 to 5 servings*

Sweet and Sour Cabbage Borscht

2 pounds boneless beef chuck roast, cut into 4 pieces
1 can (28 ounces) whole tomatoes, cut into pieces, undrained
1 can (15 ounces) tomato sauce
1 large onion, thinly sliced
3 carrots, shredded
2 pounds green cabbage, shredded
4 cups water
$\frac{3}{4}$ cup sugar
$\frac{1}{2}$ cup lemon juice
1 tablespoon caraway seeds
2 teaspoons salt
1 teaspoon black pepper

Slow Cooker Directions

1. Place all ingredients into slow cooker. Cover; cook on LOW 6 to 8 hours or until meat is tender.

2. Remove beef from slow cooker; shred. Return to slow cooker; mix well.
                                         Makes 8 to 10 servings

Italian-Style Sausage with Rice

Southwestern Stuffed Peppers

Prep Time: *15 minutes* / **Cook Time:** *4 to 6 hours*

4 green bell peppers
1 can (16 ounces) black beans, rinsed and drained
1 cup (4 ounces) shredded pepper-Jack cheese
¾ cup medium salsa
½ cup frozen corn
½ cup chopped green onions with tops
⅓ cup uncooked long grain converted rice
1 teaspoon chili powder
½ teaspoon ground cumin
Sour cream (optional)

Slow Cooker Directions

1. Cut thin slice off top of each bell pepper. Carefully remove seeds, leaving pepper whole.

2. Combine remaining ingredients except sour cream in medium bowl. Spoon filling evenly into each pepper. Place peppers in slow cooker.

3. Cover; cook on LOW 4 to 6 hours. Serve with dollop of sour cream, if desired. *Makes 4 servings*

Southwestern Stuffed Peppers

Cajun-Style Country Ribs

Prep Time: *15 minutes* / **Cook Time:** *6 to 8 hours*

- 2 cups baby carrots
- 1 large onion, coarsely chopped
- 1 large green bell pepper, cut into 1-inch pieces
- 1 large red bell pepper, cut into 1-inch pieces
- 2 teaspoons minced garlic
- 6 teaspoons Cajun or Creole seasoning, divided
- 3½ to 4 pounds pork country-style ribs
- 1 can (14½ ounces) stewed tomatoes, undrained
- 2 tablespoons water
- 1 tablespoon cornstarch
  Hot cooked rice

Slow Cooker Directions

1. Place carrots, onion, bell peppers, garlic and 2 teaspoons Cajun seasoning in slow cooker; mix well.

2. Trim excess fat from ribs. Cut into individual ribs. Sprinkle 3 teaspoons Cajun seasoning over ribs; place in slow cooker over vegetables. Pour tomatoes with juice over ribs. (Slow cooker will be full.) Cover; cook on LOW 6 to 8 hours or until ribs are fork tender.

3. Remove ribs and vegetables from cooking liquid to serving platter. Let liquid stand 5 minutes to allow fat to rise. Skim off fat. Blend water, cornstarch and remaining 1 teaspoon Cajun seasoning. Stir into liquid in slow cooker. Cook on HIGH until sauce is thickened. Return ribs and vegetables to sauce; carefully stir to coat. Serve with rice.   *Makes 6 to 8 servings*

Cajun-Style Country Ribs

Pork Meatballs & Sauerkraut

Prep Time: *30 minutes* / **Cook Time:** *6 to 8 hours*

1¼ **pounds lean ground pork**
¾ **cup dry bread crumbs**
1 **egg, lightly beaten**
2 **tablespoons milk**
2 **teaspoons caraway seeds, divided**
1 **teaspoon salt**
½ **teaspoon Worcestershire sauce**
¼ **teaspoon black pepper**
1 **bag (32 ounces) sauerkraut, drained, squeezed dry and snipped**
½ **cup chopped onion**
6 **slices bacon, crisp-cooked and crumbled**
  Chopped fresh parsley (optional)

Slow Cooker Directions

1. Combine ground pork, bread crumbs, egg, milk, 1 teaspoon caraway seeds, salt, Worcestershire and pepper in large bowl. Shape mixture into 2-inch balls. Brown meatballs in large nonstick skillet over medium-high heat.

2. Combine sauerkraut, onion, bacon and remaining 1 teaspoon caraway seeds in slow cooker. Place meatballs on top of sauerkraut mixture.

3. Cover; cook on LOW 6 to 8 hours. Garnish with parsley, if desired.

Makes 4 to 6 servings

Pork Meatballs & Sauerkraut

Layered Mexican-Style Casserole

Prep Time: *15 minutes* / **Cook Time:** *6 to 8 hours*

2 cans (15½ ounces each) hominy,* drained
1 can (15 ounces) black beans, rinsed and drained
1 can (14½ ounces) diced tomatoes with garlic, basil and oregano,
    undrained
1 cup thick and chunky salsa
1 can (6 ounces) tomato paste
½ teaspoon ground cumin
3 large flour tortillas (about 9-inch diameter)
2 cups (8 ounces) shredded Monterey Jack cheese
¼ cup sliced black olives

Hominy is corn that has been treated with slaked lime to remove the germ and hull. It can be found with the canned vegetables in most supermarkets.

Slow Cooker Directions

1. Prepare foil handles.** Spray slow cooker with nonstick cooking spray.

2. Stir together hominy, beans, tomatoes with juice, salsa, tomato paste and cumin in large bowl.

3. Press one tortilla in bottom of slow cooker. (Edges of tortilla may turn up slightly.) Top with one third of hominy mixture and one third of cheese. Repeat layers. Press remaining tortilla on top. Top with remaining hominy mixture. Set aside remaining cheese.

4. Cover; cook on LOW 6 to 8 hours. Sprinkle with remaining cheese and olives. Cover; let stand 5 minutes. Pull out tortilla stack with foil handles.

Makes 6 servings

**Tear off three 18×2-inch strips of heavy-duty foil or use regular foil folded to double thickness. Crisscross foil strips in spoke design and place into slow cooker to make lifting of tortilla stack easier.*

Layered Mexican-Style Casserole

Beef with Green Chilies

Prep Time: *15 minutes* / **Cook Time:** *7 to 8 hours*

¼ **cup plus 1 tablespoon all-purpose flour**
½ **teaspoon salt**
¼ **teaspoon black pepper**
1 **pound beef for stew**
1 **tablespoon vegetable oil**
2 **cloves garlic, minced**
1 **cup beef broth**
1 **can (7 ounces) diced mild green chilies, drained**
½ **teaspoon dried oregano leaves**
2 **tablespoons water**
  Hot cooked rice (optional)
  Diced tomato (optional)

Slow Cooker Directions

1. Combine ¼ cup flour, salt and pepper in resealable plastic food storage bag. Add beef; shake to coat beef. Heat oil in large skillet over medium-high heat. Add beef and garlic. Brown beef on all sides. Place beef mixture into slow cooker. Add broth to skillet scraping up any browned bits. Pour broth mixture into slow cooker. Add chilies and oregano.

2. Cover; cook on LOW 7 to 8 hours. For thicker sauce, combine remaining 1 tablespoon flour and water in small bowl stirring until mixture is smooth. Stir mixture into slow cooker; mix well. Cover and cook until thickened.

3. Serve with rice and garnish with diced tomato, if desired.

Makes 4 servings

COOK'S TIP

Use two cans of chilies for a slightly hotter taste.

Sweet and Sour Shrimp

Prep Time: *15 to 20 minutes* / **Cook Time:** *2 to 4½ hours*

- 1 can (16 ounces) sliced peaches in syrup, undrained
- ½ cup chopped green onions
- ½ cup chopped red bell pepper
- ½ cup chopped green bell pepper
- ½ cup chopped celery
- ⅓ cup vegetable broth
- ¼ cup light soy sauce
- 2 tablespoons rice wine vinegar
- 2 tablespoons dark sesame oil
- 1 teaspoon red pepper flakes
- 6 ounces snow peas
- 1 pound cooked medium shrimp
- 1 cup cherry tomatoes, cut into halves
- ½ cup toasted walnut pieces
- Hot cooked rice

Slow Cooker Directions

1. Place peaches with syrup, onions, bell peppers, celery, broth, soy sauce, vinegar, sesame oil and red pepper flakes in slow cooker. Cover; cook on LOW 3 to 4 hours or on HIGH 2 to 3 hours or until vegetables are tender. Stir well.

2. Add snow peas. Cook 15 minutes on HIGH. Add shrimp, tomatoes and walnuts. Cook 4 to 5 minutes on HIGH or until shrimp is hot. Serve with rice.

Makes 4 to 6 servings

SANDWICHES & WRAPS

Slow Cooker Steak Fajitas

Prep Time: *20 minutes* / **Cook Time:** *6 to 7 hours*

1 beef flank steak (about 1 pound), cut lengthwise in half, then crosswise into thin strips
1 medium onion, cut into strips
½ cup medium salsa
2 tablespoons fresh lime juice
2 tablespoons chopped fresh cilantro
2 cloves garlic, minced
1 tablespoon chili powder
1 teaspoon ground cumin
½ teaspoon salt
1 small green bell pepper, cut into strips
1 small red bell pepper, cut into strips
   Flour tortillas, warmed
   Additional salsa

Slow Cooker Directions

1. Combine steak, onion, ½ cup salsa, lime juice, cilantro, garlic, chili powder, cumin and salt in slow cooker.

2. Cover; cook on LOW 5 to 6 hours. Add bell peppers. Cover; cook on LOW 1 hour.

3. Serve with tortillas and additional salsa. *Makes 4 servings*

Barbecued Beef Sandwiches

Prep Time: *20 to 25 minutes* / **Cook Time:** *8½ to 10½ hours*

3 pounds boneless beef chuck shoulder roast, cut in half
2 cups ketchup
1 medium onion, chopped
¼ cup cider vinegar
¼ cup dark molasses
2 tablespoons Worcestershire sauce
2 cloves garlic, minced
½ teaspoon salt
½ teaspoon dry mustard
½ teaspoon black pepper
¼ teaspoon garlic powder
¼ teaspoon red pepper flakes
    Sesame seed sandwich buns, split

Slow Cooker Directions

1. Place roast in slow cooker. Combine ketchup, onion, vinegar, molasses, Worcestershire, garlic, salt, mustard, black pepper, garlic powder and red pepper flakes in large bowl. Pour sauce mixture over roast. Cover; cook on LOW 8 to 10 hours or on HIGH 4 to 5 hours.

2. Remove roast from sauce; cool slightly. Trim and discard excess fat from beef. Using two forks, shred meat.

3. Let sauce stand 5 minutes to allow fat to rise. Skim off fat.

4. Return shredded meat to slow cooker. Stir meat to evenly coat with sauce. Adjust seasonings, if desired. Cover; cook on LOW 15 to 30 minutes or until hot.

5. Spoon filling into buns and top with additional sauce, if desired.

Makes 12 servings

Barbecued Beef Sandwich

Hot & Juicy Reuben Sandwiches

Prep Time: *25 minutes* / **Cook Time:** *7 to 9 hours*

1 mild-cure corned beef (about 1½ pounds), trimmed of excess fat
2 cups sauerkraut, drained
½ cup beef broth
1 small onion, sliced
1 clove garlic, minced
¼ teaspoon caraway seeds
4 to 6 peppercorns
8 slices pumpernickel or rye bread
4 slices Swiss cheese
   Mustard

Slow Cooker Directions

1. Place corned beef, sauerkraut, broth, onion, garlic, caraway seeds and peppercorns in slow cooker.

2. Cover; cook on LOW 7 to 9 hours.

3. Remove beef from slow cooker. Cut across the grain into ¼-inch-thick slices. Divide evenly on 4 slices bread. Top each slice with ½ cup drained sauerkraut mixture and one slice cheese. Spread mustard on remaining 4 bread slices. Close sandwich.   *Makes 4 servings*

Note: This two-fisted stack of corned beef, sauerkraut and melted Swiss cheese makes a glorious sandwich you'll want to serve often.

Hot & Juicy Reuben Sandwich

Brats in Beer

Prep Time: *5 minutes* / **Cook Time:** *4 to 5 hours*

1½ **pounds bratwurst links (about 5 or 6)**
 1 **can or bottle (12 ounces) beer (not dark)**
 1 **medium onion, thinly sliced**
 2 **tablespoons packed brown sugar**
 2 **tablespoons red wine or cider vinegar**
   Mustard
   Cocktail rye bread

Slow Cooker Directions

1. Combine bratwurst, beer, medium onion, brown sugar and vinegar in slow cooker.

2. Cover; cook on LOW 4 to 5 hours.

3. Remove bratwurst from cooking liquid. Cut into ½-inch-thick slices. For mini open-faced sandwiches, spread mustard on cocktail rye bread. Top with bratwurst slices and onions from slow cooker, if desired. Arrange on platter.

Makes 30 to 36 sandwiches

COOK'S TIP

Choose a light-tasting beer for cooking
brats. Hearty ales might leave the meat
tasting slightly bitter.

Brats in Beer

Mexican-Style Shredded Beef

Prep Time: *12 minutes* / **Cook Time:** *8 to 10½ hours*

1 tablespoon ground cumin
1 tablespoon ground coriander
1 tablespoon chili powder
1 teaspoon salt
½ teaspoon ground red pepper
1 boneless beef chuck shoulder roast (about 3 pounds), cut in half
1 cup salsa or picante sauce
2 tablespoons water
1 tablespoon cornstarch

Slow Cooker Directions

1. Combine cumin, coriander, chili powder, salt and red pepper in small bowl. Rub over beef. Place ¼ cup of salsa in slow cooker; top with one piece beef. Layer ¼ cup salsa, remaining beef and ½ cup salsa in slow cooker. Cover; cook on LOW 8 to 10 hours or until meat is tender.

2. Remove beef from cooking liquid; cool slightly. Trim and discard excess fat from beef. Using two forks, shred meat.

3. Let cooking liquid stand 5 minutes to allow fat to rise. Skim off fat. To thicken liquid, blend water and cornstarch. Whisk into liquid. Cook, uncovered, on HIGH until thickened. Return beef to slow cooker. Cook 15 to 30 minutes or until hot. Adjust seasonings, if desired. Serve as meat filling for tacos, fajitas or burritos. Leftover mixture may be refrigerated up to 3 days or frozen up to 3 months. *Makes 5 cups filling*

Mexican-Style Shredded Beef

Spicy Asian Pork Filling

Prep Time: *15 to 20 minutes* / **Cook Time:** *8 to 10½ hours*

1 boneless pork sirloin roast (about 3 pounds), cut into 2- to 3-inch
    chunks
½ cup tamari or soy sauce
1 tablespoon chili garlic sauce or chili paste
2 teaspoons minced fresh ginger
2 tablespoons water
1 tablespoon cornstarch
2 teaspoons dark sesame oil

Slow Cooker Directions

1. Combine pork, tamari sauce, chili garlic sauce and ginger in slow cooker;
mix well. Cover; cook on LOW 8 to 10 hours or on HIGH 4 to 5 hours or until
pork is fork tender.

2. Remove roast from cooking liquid; cool slightly. Trim and discard excess
fat. Shred pork using 2 forks. Let liquid stand 5 minutes to allow fat to rise.
Skim off fat.

3. Blend water, cornstarch and sesame oil; whisk into liquid. Cook, uncovered,
on HIGH until thickened. Add shredded meat to slow cooker; mix well. Cook
15 to 30 minutes or until hot.   *Makes 5½ cups filling*

Spicy Asian Pork Bundles: Place ¼ cup pork filling into large lettuce leaves.
Wrap to enclose. Makes about 20 bundles.

Moo Shu Pork: Lightly spread plum sauce over warm small flour tortillas.
Spoon ¼ cup pork filling and ¼ cup stir-fried vegetables into flour tortillas.
Wrap to enclose. Serve immediately. Makes about 20 tortillas.

Spicy Asian Pork Filling

Chicken Enchilada Roll-Ups

Prep Time: *20 minutes* / **Cook Time:** *7 to 8 hours*

1½ **pounds boneless skinless chicken breasts, each cut lengthwise into 2 or 3 strips**

½ **cup plus 2 tablespoons all-purpose flour, divided**

½ **teaspoon salt**

2 **tablespoons butter**

1 **cup chicken broth**

1 **small onion, diced**

¼ **to ½ cup canned jalapeño peppers,* sliced**

½ **teaspoon dried oregano leaves**

2 **tablespoons heavy cream or milk**

6 **flour tortillas (7 to 8 inches)**

6 **thin slices American cheese or American cheese with jalapeño peppers**

*Jalapeño peppers can sting and irritate the skin; wear rubber gloves when handling peppers and do not touch eyes. Wash hands after handling.

Slow Cooker Directions

1. Combine ½ cup flour and salt in resealable plastic food storage bag. Add chicken strips and shake to coat with flour mixture. Melt butter in large skillet over medium heat. Brown chicken strips in batches 2 to 3 minutes per side. Place chicken into slow cooker.

2. Add broth to skillet and scrape up any browned bits. Pour broth mixture into slow cooker. Add onion, jalapeño peppers and oregano. Cover; cook on LOW 7 to 8 hours or on HIGH 3 to 4 hours.

3. Combine remaining 2 tablespoons flour and cream in small bowl; stir to form paste. Stir into chicken mixture; cook on HIGH until thickened. Spoon chicken mixture onto center of flour tortillas. Top with 1 cheese slice. Fold up tortillas and serve.   *Makes 6 servings*

Chicken Enchilada Roll-Up

Barbecued Pulled Pork

1 boneless pork shoulder or butt roast (3 to 4 pounds), trimmed of
   excess fat
1 teaspoon salt
1 teaspoon ground cumin
1 teaspoon paprika
1 teaspoon black pepper
1/2 teaspoon ground red pepper
1 medium onion, thinly sliced
1 medium green bell pepper, cut into strips
1 bottle (18 ounces) barbecue sauce
1/2 cup packed light brown sugar
   Sandwich rolls

Slow Cooker Directions

1. Combine salt, cumin, paprika, black pepper and red pepper in small bowl;
rub over roast.

2. Place onion and bell pepper in slow cooker; add pork. Combine barbecue
sauce and brown sugar in medium bowl; pour over meat. Cover; cook on
LOW 8 to 10 hours.

3. Transfer roast to cutting board. Trim and discard fat from roast. Using
2 forks, pull pork into coarse shreds. Serve pork with sauce on sandwich rolls.

Makes 4 to 6 servings

Barbecued Pulled Pork

Slow-Cooked Kielbasa in a Bun

Prep Time: *10 minutes* / **Cook Time:** *7 to 8 hours*

1 pound kielbasa, cut into 4 (4- to 5-inch) pieces
1 large onion, thinly sliced
1 large green bell pepper, cut into strips
¼ teaspoon salt
¼ teaspoon dried thyme leaves
¼ teaspoon black pepper
½ cup chicken broth
4 hoagie rolls, split

Slow Cooker Directions

1. Brown kielbasa in nonstick skillet over medium-high heat 3 to 4 minutes. Place kielbasa in slow cooker. Add onion, bell pepper, salt, thyme and black pepper. Stir in broth.

2. Cover; cook on LOW 7 to 8 hours.

3. Place kielbasa into rolls. Serve with favorite condiments.

Makes 4 servings

COOK'S TIP

For zesty flavor, top sandwiches with pickled peppers and a dollop of mustard.

Slow-Cooked Kielbasa in a Bun

Meatball Grinders

1 can (15 ounces) diced tomatoes, drained and juices reserved
1 can (8 ounces) no-salt-added tomato sauce
¼ cup chopped onion
2 tablespoons tomato paste
1 teaspoon dried Italian seasoning
1 pound ground chicken
½ cup fresh whole wheat or white bread crumbs (1 slice bread)
1 egg white, lightly beaten
3 tablespoons finely chopped fresh parsley
2 cloves garlic, minced
¼ teaspoon salt
⅛ teaspoon black pepper
  Nonstick cooking spray
4 small hard rolls, split
2 tablespoons grated Parmesan cheese

Slow Cooker Directions

1. Combine diced tomatoes, ½ cup reserved juice, tomato sauce, onion, tomato paste and Italian seasoning in slow cooker. Cover; cook on LOW 3 to 4 hours or until onions are soft.

2. Halfway through cooking time, prepare meatballs. Combine chicken, bread crumbs, egg white, parsley, garlic, salt and pepper in medium bowl. With wet hands, form mixture into 12 to 16 meatballs. Spray medium nonstick skillet with cooking spray; heat over medium heat until hot. Add meatballs; cook about 8 to 10 minutes or until well browned on all sides. Remove meatballs to slow cooker; cook on LOW 1 to 2 hours or until meatballs are no longer pink in centers and are heated through.

3. Place 3 to 4 meatballs in each roll. Spoon sauce over meatballs. Sprinkle with cheese. *Makes 4 servings*

Meatball Grinder

Fiery Chili Beef

Prep Time: *15 minutes* / **Cook Time:** *7 to 8 hours*

1 beef flank steak (1 to 1½ pounds), cut into 6 evenly-sized pieces
1 can (28 ounces) diced tomatoes, undrained
1 can (15 ounces) pinto beans, rinsed and drained
1 medium onion, chopped
2 cloves garlic, minced
½ teaspoon salt
½ teaspoon ground cumin
¼ teaspoon black pepper
1 canned chipotle chile pepper in adobo sauce,* diced and 1 teaspoon
    adobo sauce, reserved
  Flour tortillas

Chile peppers can sting and irritate the skin; wear rubber gloves when handling peppers and do not touch eyes. Wash hands after handling.

Slow Cooker Directions

1. Combine steak, tomatoes with juice, beans, onion, garlic, salt, cumin and black pepper in slow cooker.

2. Add pepper and adobo sauce to slow cooker; mix well.

3. Cover; cook on LOW 7 to 8 hours. Serve with tortillas.

Makes 6 servings

COOK'S TIP

Chipotle chile peppers are dried, smoked
jalapeño peppers with a very hot yet smoky,
sweet flavor. They can be found dried, pickled
and canned in adobo sauce.

Fiery Chili Beef

Shredded Apricot Pork Sandwiches

2 medium onions, thinly sliced

1 cup apricot preserves

1/2 cup packed dark brown sugar

1/2 cup barbecue sauce

1/4 cup cider vinegar

2 tablespoons Worcestershire sauce

1/2 teaspoon red pepper flakes

1 (4-pound) boneless pork top loin roast or pork shoulder roast,
   trimmed of fat

1/4 cup cold water

2 tablespoons cornstarch

1 tablespoon grated fresh ginger

1 teaspoon salt

1 teaspoon black pepper

10 to 12 sesame or onion rolls, toasted

Slow Cooker Directions

1. Combine onions, preserves, brown sugar, barbecue sauce, vinegar, Worcestershire sauce and red pepper flakes in small bowl. Place pork roast in slow cooker. Pour apricot mixture over roast. Cover; cook on LOW 8 to 9 hours.

2. Remove pork from cooking liquid to cutting board; cool slightly. Using 2 forks, shred pork into coarse shreds. Let liquid stand 5 minutes to allow fat to rise. Skim fat.

3. Combine water, cornstarch, ginger, salt and black pepper; blend well. Whisk cornstarch mixture into slow cooker liquid. Cook, covered, on HIGH 15 to 30 minutes or until thickened. Return shredded pork to slow cooker; mix well. Serve in toasted rolls.   *Makes 10 to 12 sandwiches*

Shredded Apricot Pork Sandwich

Hot Chicken Baguettes

Prep Time: *15 minutes /* **Cook Time:** *5 to 6 hours*

1 to 2 carrots, sliced

½ cup sliced celery

1 small onion, chopped

1 clove garlic, minced

¼ teaspoon dried oregano leaves

¼ teaspoon red pepper flakes

¼ cup all-purpose flour

1 teaspoon salt

   Black pepper

6 boneless skinless chicken thighs or breasts, trimmed of all visible fat

1 can (14½ ounces) chicken broth

6 small French bread baguettes, split and toasted

6 slices Swiss cheese (optional)

Slow Cooker Directions

1. Place carrots, celery, onion, garlic, oregano and red pepper flakes in slow cooker.

2. Combine flour, salt and black pepper in large resealable plastic food storage bag. Add chicken, 2 pieces at a time; shake to coat. Heat oil in large skillet over medium-high heat. Add chicken; brown about 2 minutes on each side.

3. Place chicken over vegetables in slow cooker; add broth. Cover; cook 5 to 6 hours on LOW or until chicken is tender.

4. Place 1 piece chicken on bottom half of each baguette. Spoon 1 to 2 tablespoons broth mixture over chicken. Top with 1 slice cheese, if desired. Close baguette. *Makes 6 servings*

Spicy Beef and Pepper Fajitas

Prep Time: *10 minutes* / **Cook Time:** *8 to 10 hours*

1 beef flank steak (about 1¹/₂ pounds), cut into 6 pieces
1 cup chopped onion
2 green bell peppers, cut into ¹/₂-inch-wide strips
1 jalapeño pepper,* chopped
2 tablespoons chopped fresh cilantro
2 cloves garlic, minced
1 teaspoon chili powder
1 teaspoon ground cumin
¹/₂ teaspoon salt
¹/₄ teaspoon ground red pepper
1 can (8 ounces) chopped tomatoes, drained
12 (8-inch) flour tortillas
Toppings, such as sour cream, shredded Cheddar cheese and salsa
Sliced avocado (optional)

Jalapeño peppers can sting and irritate the skin; wear rubber gloves when handling peppers and do not touch eyes. Wash hands after handling.

Slow Cooker Directions

1. Combine beef, onion, bell peppers, jalapeño pepper, cilantro, garlic, chili powder, cumin, salt and ground red pepper in slow cooker. Add tomatoes. Cover; cook on LOW 8 to 10 hours.

2. Remove beef from slow cooker and pull into shreds with fork. Return beef to slow cooker. To serve, layer beef mixture on tortillas. Top with toppings; roll up tortillas. Serve with sliced avocado, if desired.   *Makes 12 servings*

Hot Beef Sandwiches

1 chuck beef roast (3 to 4 pounds), cut into chunks
1 small jar (6 ounces) sliced dill pickles, undrained
1 medium onion, peeled and diced
1 teaspoon mustard seeds
4 cloves garlic, minced
1 can (14 ounces) crushed tomatoes with Italian seasoning
   Hamburger buns

Slow Cooker Directions

1. Place beef in slow cooker. Pour pickles with juice over top of beef. Add onion, mustard seed, garlic and tomatoes.

2. Cover; cook on LOW 8 to 10 hours.

3. Remove beef from slow cooker. Shred beef with two forks; return beef to tomato mixture; mix well. Serve beef mixture on buns.

Makes 6 to 8 servings

Serving Suggestion: Pile this beef onto a toasted roll or bun, and you'll have an out-of-this world sandwich! Garnish with lettuce, sliced tomatoes, Bermuda red onion, shredded slaw or other fixings to taste.

Hot Beef Sandwich

Chipotle Taco Filling

2 pounds ground beef chuck

2 cups chopped yellow onion

2 cans (15 ounces each) pinto beans, rinsed and drained

1 can (14½ ounces) diced tomatoes with peppers and onions, drained

4 chipotle peppers in adobo sauce, mashed

1 tablespoon beef bouillon granules

1 tablespoon sugar

1½ teaspoons ground cumin

Taco shells or flour tortillas

Toppings: shredded lettuce, salsa, shredded cheese and sour cream (optional)

Slow Cooker Directions

1. Brown ground beef in large nonstick skillet over medium-high heat, stirring to separate meat. Drain and discard fat.

2. Combine beef, onion, beans, tomatoes, peppers, bouillon, sugar and cumin in slow cooker. Cover; cook on LOW 4 hours or on HIGH 2 hours.

3. Serve in taco shells. Add shredded lettuce, salsa, shredded cheese and sour cream, if desired. *Makes 8 cups filling*

Chipotle Taco Filling

SWEETS & WARM DRINKS

Cran-Apple Orange Conserve

Prep Time: *12 minutes* / **Cook Time:** *6 to 8 hours*

   2 medium oranges
   5 large tart apples, peeled, cored and chopped
   2 cups sugar
1½ cups fresh cranberries
   1 tablespoon grated fresh lemon peel
     Pound cake

Slow Cooker Directions

1. Remove thin slice from both ends of oranges for easier chopping. Finely chop 2 cups unpeeled oranges; remove any seeds. Combine oranges, apples, sugar, cranberries and lemon peel in slow cooker. Cover; cook on HIGH 4 hours. Slightly crush fruit with potato masher.

2. Cook, uncovered, on LOW 4 hours or on HIGH 2 to 2½ hours or until very thick, stirring occasionally to prevent sticking.

3. Cool at least 2 hours. Serve with pound cake.   *Makes about 5 cups*

Serving Suggestion: Fruit conserve can also be served with roast pork or poultry.

Peach-Pecan Upside-Down Cake

Prep Time: *10 minutes* / **Cook Time:** *3 hours*

- **1 can (8½ ounces) peach slices**
- **⅓ cup packed brown sugar**
- **2 tablespoons butter or margarine, melted**
- **¼ cup chopped pecans**
- **1 package (16 ounces) pound cake mix, plus ingredients to prepare mix**
- **½ teaspoon almond extract**
- **Whipped cream (optional)**

Slow Cooker Directions

1. Generously grease 7½-inch slow cooker bread-and-cake bake pan or casserole dish; set aside.

2. Drain peach slices, reserving 1 tablespoon juice. Combine brown sugar, butter and reserved peach juice in prepared bake pan. Arrange peach slices on top of brown sugar mixture. Sprinkle with pecans.

3. Prepare cake mix according to package directions; stir in almond extract. Spread over peach mixture. Cover pan. Make foil handles* for easier removal of pan from slow cooker. Place pan into slow cooker. Cover; cook on HIGH 3 hours.

4. Use foil handles to remove pan from slow cooker. Cool, uncovered, on wire rack 10 minutes. Run narrow spatula around sides of pan; invert onto serving plate. Serve warm with whipped cream, if desired.

Makes 10 servings

*To make foil handles, tear off 3 (18×2-inch) strips heavy-duty aluminum foil or use regular foil folded to double thickness. Crisscross foil strips in spoke design and place pan on center of strips. Pull foil strips up and over pan.

Peach-Pecan Upside-Down Cake

Pineapple Daiquiri Sundae

1 pineapple, cored, peeled and cut into ½-inch chunks
½ cup *each* sugar and dark rum
3 tablespoons lime juice
 Peel of 2 limes, cut into long strands
1 tablespoon cornstarch or arrowroot
 Ice cream, pound cake or shortcakes
 Fresh raspberries and mint leaves (optional)

Slow Cooker Directions

Place first 5 ingredients in slow cooker; mix well. Cover; cook on HIGH 3 to 4 hours. Serve hot over ice cream. Garnish with raspberries and mint leaves, if desired. *Makes 4 to 6 servings*

Variation: Substitute 1 can (20 ounces) crushed pineapple, drained, for the fresh pineapple. Cook on HIGH 3 hours.

Warm & Spicy Fruit Punch

4 cinnamon sticks, broken into pieces
 Strips of 1 orange peel
1 teaspoon whole allspice
½ teaspoon whole cloves
7 cups water
1 can (12 ounces) frozen cranberry-raspberry juice concentrate, thawed
1 can (6 ounces) frozen lemonade concentrate, thawed
2 cans (5½ ounces each) apricot nectar
 Juice of 1 orange

Slow Cooker Directions

1. Tie cinnamon, orange peel, allspice and cloves in cheesecloth bag.

2. Combine water, concentrates, nectar and orange juice in slow cooker; add spice bag. Cover; cook on LOW 5 to 6 hours.

3. Remove and discard spice bag. *Makes about 14 (6-ounce) servings*

Pineapple Daiquiri Sundae

Baked Fudge Pudding Cake

¼ **cup plus 2 tablespoons unsweetened cocoa powder**
¼ **cup all-purpose flour**
⅛ **teaspoon salt**
 4 **eggs**
1⅓ **cups sugar**
 1 **cup (2 sticks) unsalted butter, melted**
 1 **teaspoon vanilla**
   Peel of 1 orange
½ **cup heavy cream**
   Chopped toasted pecans
   Whipped cream or vanilla ice cream (optional)

Slow Cooker Directions

1. Spray inside of slow cooker with nonstick cooking spray. Set slow cooker to LOW setting. Combine cocoa, flour and salt in small bowl; set aside.

2. Beat eggs with electric mixer at medium-high speed until thickened. Gradually add sugar; beat 5 minutes or until very thick and lemon-colored. Mix in butter, vanilla and orange peel. Stir cocoa mixture into egg mixture. Add heavy cream; mix until combined. Pour batter into slow cooker.

3. Before placing lid on slow cooker, cover opening with paper towel to collect condensation, making sure it does not touch pudding mixture. (Large slow cookers might require 2 connected paper towels.) Place lid over paper towel. Cook on LOW 3 to 4 hours. (Do not cook on HIGH.) Sprinkle with pecans; serve with whipped cream, if desired. Refrigerate leftovers.

Makes 6 to 8 servings

Note: Store leftover cake in a covered container in the refrigerator. To serve leftover cake, reheat individual servings in the microwave for about 15 seconds. Or, make truffles by rolling leftover cake into small balls and dipping them into melted chocolate. Let sit until chocolate hardens.

Baked Fudge Pudding Cake

Cherry Flan

Prep Time: *10 minutes* / **Cook Time:** *3½ to 4 hours*

  5 **eggs**
½ **cup sugar**
½ **teaspoon salt**
¾ **cup flour**
  1 **can (12 ounces) evaporated milk**
  1 **teaspoon vanilla**
  1 **bag (16 ounces) frozen, pitted dark sweet cherries, thawed**
     Sweetened whipped cream or cherry vanilla ice cream (optional)

Slow Cooker Directions

1. Grease inside of slow cooker.

2. Beat eggs, sugar and salt in large bowl with electric mixer at high speed until thick. Add flour; stir until smooth. Stir in evaporated milk and vanilla.

3. Pour batter into prepared slow cooker. Place cherries evenly over batter. Cover; cook on LOW 3½ to 4 hours or until flan is set. Serve warm with whipped cream, if desired.   *Makes 6 servings*

COOK'S TIP

This yummy dessert is like a custard
and a cake mixed together.

Cherry Flan

Chunky Sweet Spiced Apple Butter

4 cups (about 1¼ pounds) peeled, chopped Granny Smith apples
¾ cup packed dark brown sugar
2 tablespoons balsamic vinegar
¼ cup butter, divided
1 tablespoon ground cinnamon
½ teaspoon salt
¼ teaspoon ground cloves
1½ teaspoons vanilla

Slow Cooker Directions

1. Combine apples, sugar, vinegar, 2 tablespoons butter, cinnamon, salt and cloves in slow cooker. Cover; cook on LOW 8 hours.

2. Stir in remaining 2 tablespoons butter and vanilla. Cool completely.

Makes 2 cups

Serving Suggestions: Serve with roasted meats or on toasted English muffins.

Viennese Coffee

3 cups strong freshly brewed hot coffee
3 tablespoons chocolate syrup
1 teaspoon sugar
⅓ cup heavy cream
¼ cup crème de cacao or Irish cream (optional)
Whipped cream
Chocolate shavings for garnish

Slow Cooker Directions

1. Combine coffee, chocolate syrup and sugar in slow cooker. Cover; cook on LOW 2 to 2½ hours. Stir in heavy cream and crème de cacao, if desired. Cover; cook 30 minutes or until heated through.

2. Ladle coffee into coffee cups, top with whipped cream and chocolate shavings.

Makes about 4 servings

Chunky Sweet Spiced Apple Butter

Mulled Cranberry Tea

Prep Time: *10 minutes* / **Cook Time:** *2 to 3 hours*

2 tea bags
1 cup boiling water
1 bottle (48 ounces) cranberry juice
½ cup dried cranberries (optional)
⅓ cup sugar
1 large lemon, cut into ¼-inch slices
4 cinnamon sticks
6 whole cloves
   Additional thin lemon slices for garnish
   Additional cinnamon sticks for garnish

Slow Cooker Directions

1. Place tea bags in slow cooker. Pour boiling water over tea bags; cover and let stand 5 minutes. Remove and discard tea bags. Stir in cranberry juice, cranberries, if desired, sugar, lemon slices, 4 cinnamon sticks and cloves. Cover; cook on LOW 2 to 3 hours or on HIGH 1 to 2 hours.

2. Remove and discard lemon slices, cinnamon sticks and cloves. Serve in warm mug with additional fresh lemon slice and cinnamon stick.   *Makes 8 servings*

Chunky Vanilla Pears

1¼ pounds ripe pears, peeled and diced
8 dried orange essence plums, cut into quarters
¼ cup granulated sugar
1 tablespoon lemon juice
½ teaspoon vanilla

Slow Cooker Directions

1. Combine all ingredients except vanilla in slow cooker. Cover; cook 1 hour on HIGH.

2. Stir in vanilla. Serve hot or at room temperature with roasted ham, pork, chicken or lamb. Or, serve as dessert sauce over ice cream, angel food cake or pound cake.   *Makes 2 cups*

Mulled Cranberry Tea

Chai Tea

Prep Time: *8 minutes* / **Cook Time:** *2 to 2½ hours*

- 2 quarts (8 cups) water
- 8 bags black tea
- ¾ cup sugar*
- 16 whole cloves
- 16 whole cardamom seeds, pods removed (optional)
- 5 cinnamon sticks
- 8 slices fresh ginger
- 1 cup milk

Chai Tea is typically a sweet drink. For less sweet tea, reduce sugar to ½ cup.

Slow Cooker Directions

1. Combine water, tea, sugar, cloves, cardamom, if desired, cinnamon sticks and ginger in slow cooker. Cover; cook on HIGH 2 to 2½ hours.

2. Strain mixture; discard solids. (At this point, tea may be covered and refrigerated up to 3 days.)

3. Stir in milk just before serving. Serve warm or chilled.

Makes 8 to 10 servings

Hot Mulled Cider

- ½ gallon apple cider
- ½ cup packed light brown sugar
- ½ cup applejack or bourbon (optional)
- 1½ teaspoons balsamic or cider vinegar
- 1 teaspoon vanilla
- 1 cinnamon stick
- 6 whole cloves

Slow Cooker Directions

Combine all ingredients in slow cooker. Cover; cook on LOW 5 to 6 hours. Remove and discard cinnamon stick and cloves. Serve hot in mugs.

Makes 16 servings

Chai Tea

Steamed Pumpkin Cake

Prep Time: *15 minutes* / **Cook Time:** *3 to 3½ hours*

1½ cups all-purpose flour
1½ teaspoons baking powder
1½ teaspoons baking soda
 1 teaspoon ground cinnamon
½ teaspoon salt
¼ teaspoon ground cloves
½ cup (1 stick) unsalted butter, melted
 2 cups packed light brown sugar
 3 eggs, lightly beaten
 1 can (15 ounces) solid-pack pumpkin
   Sweetened whipped cream (optional)

Slow Cooker Directions

1. Grease 2½-quart soufflé dish or baking pan that fits into slow cooker.

2. Combine flour, baking powder, baking soda, cinnamon, salt and cloves in medium bowl; set aside.

3. Beat butter, brown sugar and eggs in large bowl with electric mixer at medium speed until creamy. Beat in pumpkin. Stir in flour mixture. Spoon batter into prepared soufflé dish.

4. Fill slow cooker with 1 inch hot water. Make foil handles* for easy removal of soufflé dish. Place soufflé dish into slow cooker. Cover; cook on HIGH 3 to 3½ hours or until wooden toothpick inserted into center comes out clean.

5. Use foil handles to lift dish from slow cooker. Cool 15 minutes. Invert cake onto serving platter. Cut into wedges and serve with dollop of whipped cream, if desired.   *Makes 12 servings*

Tear off three 18×2-inch strips of heavy foil or use regular foil folded to double thickness. Crisscross foil strips in spoke design and place soufflé dish on center of strips. Pull foil strips up and over dish.

Serving Suggestion: Enhance this old-fashioned dense cake with a topping of sautéed apples or pear slices, or a scoop of pumpkin ice cream.

Steamed Pumpkin Cake

Gingered Pineapple and Cranberries

2 cans (20 ounces each) pineapple chunks in juice, undrained
1 cup dried sweetened cranberries
½ cup brown sugar
1 teaspoon curry powder, divided
1 teaspoon grated fresh ginger, divided
¼ teaspoon red pepper flakes
2 tablespoons water
1 tablespoon cornstarch

Slow Cooker Directions

1. Place pineapple with juice, cranberries, brown sugar, ½ teaspoon curry powder, ½ teaspoon ginger and red pepper flakes into slow cooker.

2. Cover; cook on HIGH 3 hours.

3. Combine water, cornstarch, remaining ½ teaspoon curry powder and ½ teaspoon ginger in small bowl; stir until cornstarch is dissolved. Add to pineapple mixture; cook on HIGH 15 minutes or until thickened. Serve with ham, pork, chicken or lamb. Or serve over ice cream, angel food cake or pound cake. *Makes 4½ cups*

Spiced Apple Tea

3 bags cinnamon herbal tea
3 cups boiling water
2 cups unsweetened apple juice
6 whole cloves
1 cinnamon stick

Slow Cooker Directions

Place tea bags in slow cooker. Pour boiling water over tea bags; cover and let stand 10 minutes. Remove and discard tea bags. Add apple juice, cloves and cinnamon stick to slow cooker. Cover; cook on LOW 2 to 3 hours. Remove and discard cloves and cinnamon stick. Serve warm in mugs.

Makes 4 servings

Gingered Pineapple and Cranberries

Mocha Supreme

8 cups strong brewed coffee
½ cup instant hot chocolate beverage mix
1 cinnamon stick, broken into halves
1 cup whipping cream
1 tablespoon powdered sugar

Slow Cooker Directions

1. Place coffee, hot chocolate mix and cinnamon stick halves in slow cooker; stir. Cover; cook on HIGH 2 to 2½ hours or until hot. Remove and discard cinnamon stick halves.

2. Beat cream in medium bowl with electric mixer at high speed until soft peaks form. Add powdered sugar; beat until stiff peaks form. Ladle hot beverage into mugs; top with whipped cream. *Makes 8 servings*

COOK'S TIP

You can whip cream faster if you first chill the beaters and bowls in the freezer for 15 minutes.

Mocha Supreme

"Peachy Keen" Dessert Treat

1⅓ cups uncooked old-fashioned oats
1 cup granulated sugar
1 cup packed light brown sugar
⅔ cup buttermilk baking mix
2 teaspoons ground cinnamon
½ teaspoon ground nutmeg
2 pounds fresh peaches (about 8 medium), sliced

Slow Cooker Directions

Combine oats, sugars, baking mix, cinnamon and nutmeg in large bowl. Stir in peaches; mix until well blended. Pour mixture into slow cooker. Cover; cook on LOW 4 to 6 hours. *Makes 8 to 12 servings*

Spiced Plums and Pears

2 cans (29 ounces each) sliced pears in heavy syrup, undrained
2 pounds black or red plums (about 12 to 14), pitted and sliced
1 cup packed brown sugar
1 teaspoon ground cinnamon
½ teaspoon ground ginger
¼ teaspoon grated lemon peel
2 tablespoons cornstarch
2 tablespoons water
Pound cake or ice cream
Whipped topping

Slow Cooker Directions

1. Cut pear slices in half. Place pears with syrup, plums, sugar, cinnamon, ginger and lemon peel in slow cooker. Cover; cook on HIGH 4 hours.

2. Combine cornstarch and water to make smooth paste. Stir into slow cooker. Cook on HIGH until slightly thickened.

3. Serve warm or at room temperature over pound cake with whipped topping, or serve as condiment with baked ham, roast pork or turkey.

Makes 6 to 8 servings

"Peachy Keen" Dessert Treat

Apple-Date Crisp

6 cups thinly sliced peeled apples (about 6 medium apples, preferably
  Golden Delicious)
2 teaspoons lemon juice
⅓ cup chopped dates
1⅓ cups uncooked quick oats
½ cup all-purpose flour
½ cup packed light brown sugar
½ teaspoon ground cinnamon
¼ teaspoon salt
¼ teaspoon ground ginger
  Dash ground nutmeg
  Dash ground cloves (optional)
¼ cup (½ stick) cold butter, cut into small pieces

Slow Cooker Directions

1. Spray slow cooker with nonstick cooking spray. Place apples in medium bowl. Sprinkle with lemon juice; toss to coat. Add dates; mix well. Transfer apple mixture to slow cooker.

2. Combine oats, flour, brown sugar, cinnamon, salt, ginger, nutmeg and cloves, if desired, in medium bowl. Cut in butter with pastry blender or two knives until mixture resembles coarse crumbs.

3. Sprinkle oat mixture over apples; smooth top. Cover; cook on LOW about 4 hours or on HIGH about 2 hours or until apples are tender.

Makes 6 servings

Apple-Date Crisp

Chocolate Chip Lemon Loaf

¾ **cup granulated sugar**
½ **cup shortening**
2 **eggs, lightly beaten**
1⅔ **cups all-purpose flour**
1½ **teaspoons baking powder**
¼ **teaspoon salt**
¾ **cup milk**
½ **cup chocolate chips**
 Strips of 1 lemon peel
 Juice of 1 lemon
¼ **to** ½ **cup powdered sugar**
 Melted chocolate (optional)

Slow Cooker Directions

1. Grease 2-quart soufflé dish or 2-pound coffee can; set aside. Beat granulated sugar and shortening until blended. Add eggs, one at a time, mixing well after each addition.

2. Sift together flour, baking powder and salt. Add flour mixture and milk alternately to shortening mixture. Stir in chocolate chips and lemon peel.

3. Spoon batter into prepared dish. Cover with greased foil. Place in preheated slow cooker. Cook, covered, with slow cooker lid slightly ajar to allow excess moisture to escape, on LOW 3 to 4 hours or on HIGH 1¾ to 2 hours or until edges are golden and knife inserted into center of loaf comes out clean. Remove dish from slow cooker; remove foil. Place loaf on wire rack to cool completely.

4. Combine lemon juice and ¼ cup powdered sugar in small bowl. Add more sugar as needed to reach desired consistency. Pour glaze over loaf. Drizzle loaf with melted chocolate, if desired. *Makes 8 servings*

Chocolate Chip Lemon Loaf

Orangey Date-Nut Bread

2 cups all-purpose unbleached flour
1 teaspoon baking powder
½ teaspoon baking soda
¼ teaspoon salt
½ cup chopped pecans
1 cup chopped dates
2 teaspoons dried orange peel
⅔ cup boiling water
¾ cup sugar
2 tablespoons shortening
1 egg, lightly beaten
1 teaspoon vanilla

Slow Cooker Directions

1. Spray 1-quart baking pan, soufflé dish or other baking pan with high sides with nonstick cooking spray; dust with flour. Set aside.

2. Combine flour, baking powder, baking soda, salt and pecans in medium bowl; set aside.

3. Combine dates and orange peel in separate medium bowl; pour boiling water over date mixture. Add sugar, shortening, egg and vanilla; stir just until combined.

4. Add flour mixture to date mixture; stir just until combined. Pour batter into prepared pan. Place pan in slow cooker. Cover; cook on HIGH about 2½ hours or until edges begin to brown.

5. Remove pan from slow cooker. Cool on wire rack about 10 minutes; remove bread from pan and cool completely on rack.

Makes 8 to 10 servings

Variation: Substitute 1 cup dried cranberries for dates.

Pumpkin Custard

1 cup solid-pack pumpkin
½ cup packed brown sugar
2 eggs, beaten
½ teaspoon ground ginger
½ teaspoon ground cinnamon
½ teaspoon grated lemon peel
1 can (12 ounces) evaporated milk
Additional ground cinnamon

Slow Cooker Directions

1. Combine pumpkin, brown sugar, eggs, ginger, cinnamon and lemon peel in large bowl. Stir in evaporated milk. Pour mixture into 1½-quart soufflé dish. Cover tightly with foil.

2. Make foil handles.* Place soufflé dish in slow cooker. Pour water into slow cooker to come about 1½ inches from top of soufflé dish. Cover; cook on LOW 4 hours.

3. Use foil handles to lift dish from slow cooker. Sprinkle with additional ground cinnamon. Serve warm.   *Makes 6 servings*

*To make foil handles, tear off three 18×3-inch strips of heavy-duty foil. Crisscross the strips so they resemble the spokes of a wheel. Place the dish or food in the center of the strips. Pull the foil strips up and over and place into the slow cooker. Leave them in while you cook so you can easily lift the item out again when ready.

INDEX